MR T

does

PRIMARY
HISTORY

MR T

does

PRIMARY HISTORY

STUART TIFFANY

Mr T Does Primary History

CORWIN

A Sage company
2455 Teller Road
Thousand Oaks, California 91320
(0800)233-9936
www.corwin.com

Sage
1 Oliver's Yard
55 City Road
London EC1Y 1SP

Sage
B 1/l 1 Mohan Cooperative Industrial Area
Mathura Road
New Delhi 110 044

Sage
3 Church Street
#10-04 Samsung Hub
Singapore 049483

First edition published in 2023

Editor: Amy Thornton
Senior project editor: Chris Marke
Marketing manager: Dilhara Attygalle
Cover design: Wendy Scott
Typeset by: C&M Digitals (P) Ltd, Chennai, India
Printed in the UK

Library of Congress Control Number: 2023930609

British Library Cataloguing in Publication Data

A catalogue record for this book is available from the British Library.

ISBN 978-1-5296-1103-8
ISBN 978-1-5296-1102-1 (pbk)

At Sage we take sustainability seriously. Most of our products are printed in the UK using responsibly sourced papers and boards. When we print overseas we ensure sustainable papers are used as measured by the Book Chain Project grading system. We undertake an annual audit to monitor our sustainability.

CONTENTS

ACKNOWLEDGEMENTS

Writing this book has been a wonderful opportunity to reflect on both who and what has shaped my perspective on history teaching and general worldview. There are so many people I'd like to thank for this or their help and guidance on writing the book.

First, without those early family outings, this passionate nerdery would have been harder to trace so Mum, Dad, Grandma, Grandad and my exploring colleague and brother Matt, North Wales holidays were awesome!

In a school sense, two teachers stand out and get a mention in Chapter 1. My lovely year 4 teacher and secondary history teacher were a huge influence.

When I think about my approach as a teacher, I owe so much to Bev Forrest of Leeds Trinity. I'm blessed to call her not only a colleague but a mentor and friend. The team at Westroyd Primary School and Nursery have been my guinea pigs in developing many of these ideas and shaped the content and my positive attitude. The power of teachers should never, ever be underestimated.

Last, but definitely not least, the staff and primary committee members at the Historical Association do an incredible job supporting history teachers.

Thanks to you for taking the time to read this.

ABOUT THE AUTHOR

Stuart Tiffany is an experienced primary school teacher, history specialist, visiting lecturer, CPD provider and member of the Historical Association's primary committee since 2018. He has worked at a number of schools as a teacher and subject leader across West Yorkshire. He now supports schools nationwide on developing their curriculum offer and upskilling staff on history as a subject discipline. He runs the largest primary history-focused page on Facebook (www.facebook.com/MrTdoesPrimaryHistory) with a simple aim of offering free advice and support to anyone that reaches out and sharing the best practice in primary history. This has grown into a business that takes him nationwide sharing the absolute joy that primary history can bring through virtual and in-person inset and twilight CPD sessions.

ABOUT THIS BOOK

This book will help guide teachers through an approach to building a unit of work. It involves four deliberately sequenced phases which focus on ensuring children can learn the core substantive and disciplinary knowledge as they progress through historical enquiries. It discusses several factors which play a role when selecting which historical narratives a teacher can choose to teach while still meeting the curriculum specification. Alongside this, two units of work exemplify what the tangible 'product' could look like in the classroom. This is to provide as much clarity as possible to support fellow teachers in making the most of the primary history curriculum.

While I will be making use of several pieces of research, this book isn't a compendium of it. The research I use is that which has impacted the way in which I think about, plan and teach history. When these pieces are explained, it will be in that specific context even though the principles have wide-reaching ramifications across the curriculum.

Also, the book isn't just a series of lesson ideas; it contains core principles which are applicable across the entire history curriculum. Questions are posed to suggest when and how to reflect on the nature of the current provision. Then, consideration is given to how amendments could be included and why that may be beneficial. I would never be so bold as to claim this is *the* way to teach history. There is a multitude of approaches which can yield success when placed alongside supporting pedagogy. This is the way in which I approach planning and the merits of that hopefully come across. If there is one lesson I have learned since starting as a teacher, it's that each teacher has their own style and pedagogy. Blend what is included in the book with how you run your classroom to make it meaningful for you.

My prime aim in writing this book is to help teachers realise how brilliant primary history teaching is and support them in understanding the rich possibilities contained within the National Curriculum 2014. I'll refer to mistakes I have made in the past to explain how and why I now teach in a different way.

Ultimately though, this book is designed to make teachers think. It's designed to make teachers think about what they teach, why they teach it and the value that knowing more and remembering more about the past brings to the students they teach.

1

WHY I LOVE HISTORY

BEFORE WE START ...

Take a minute and think about history in your mind.

- Do you like it?
- What memories do you have of it?
- Are there any moments that shape the way you teach it?

WHERE MY LOVE OF HISTORY HAS COME FROM

Ever since I was a small child, I've been fascinated by the ruined remains of the past. Many hours were spent charging around the castles of North Wales, abbeys of North Yorkshire and all the museums that would distract my brother and me for a day during the school holidays. I said something immensely cringy around the age of nine to my grandad which he doesn't let me forget: 'You know, Grandad. History is my passion!' – so I can officially say that I have been an enormous history nerd ... enthusiast ... geek from a very young age.

The thing that really captured my imagination is what these ruined sites were, how and why Sandal castle in West Yorkshire came to be a hill with several outcrops of rocks and why it was so different to Harlech or Caernarfon that look relatively unchanged. I'm not going to pretend that I was a child who stopped and read all the signs and information points – that would be a shameless lie! – but what always stuck with me is that connection to the past. If you take a walk for ten minutes in most places, you pass so many incredible sites and stories that offer an insight into the past.

When teaching, it can be such a challenge to present something that may appear so mundane to a generation of children that have sights and sounds in their faces 24 hours a day. This doesn't mean we resort to gimmicks and potentially misrepresentative lessons but rather immerse them into these ancient worlds ... the stories of how, when and where developments that shaped 21st-century life took place.

My great aunt was a secondary languages teacher and keen local historian as well. She could talk so eloquently about her research into genealogy and the way it helped her tell the stories of my family's past. She was the person that took us to Sandal castle's remains and tried to explain its heritage and what it could tell us. At the time, I didn't realise the profound impact these stories were having on me but, upon subsequent reflection, they shaped the way I like to convey history while teaching – narrating the past is key. History has the word 'story' in it for a reason!

Some of my favourite school memories are from history lessons: from visiting Oakwell Hall, for example, as part of a Tudor topic to learn more about the history of the building and lives of people that may have lived in such grand surroundings. There still exist photos of me wearing a ruffle from that day made dutifully by my lovely Year 4 teacher.

This carried on through to GCSE and A level history where the focus was on the turmoil in Europe from German unification in 1871 to Stalin's Russia, Weimar Germany and Hitler's rise to power. As I learned more, the power of knowing the past became clearer: the connections between events both corelative and causal; the fact history seemingly repeats itself and those immense turning points that shape the 21st-century world in which we teach. I'm immensely grateful to the teachers that have helped me with this and I'm happy I was able to thank them for it. It's why the profession of teacher will always be significant.

I'm sure if you asked my teachers or family what I was like as a child, they would say a pain. Every time I encounter something, I have a habit of asking questions aloud even when I probably should maintain an internal monologue. Questioning helps us make sense of the world around us and is a core principle in history. A great question unlocks purposeful knowledge and helps us understand the world in ever increasing depth. Different questions stimulate different lines of enquiry and can help us piece together the nuanced, complex, contradictory world that we call history.

Whenever I visit anywhere, I spend an enormous amount of time thinking about which buildings and landmarks I can visit. Even though I'm not religious in the slightest, churches and cathedrals are invariably on my list. When I visited Rome for my birthday, I was in awe at how my memory brought to life what I'd learned and could see in front of me. Standing on Palatine Hill thinking – who has stood here before me? Am I walking in the footsteps of an emperor? Which plans were hatched in this remarkable city? Although I knew I'd never know for sure, it didn't stop it being a magical moment where those rich and complex narratives we call history came to life once again for me. The sheer opulence of St Peter's Basilica is something else. I cannot express in words the experience of walking through the enormous doorway into this symbol of immense wealth, power and significance through time. It made me think of the Vatican's role as more than just religious but societal, cultural, political and economic.

Rarely am I speechless but Le Domus Romane di Palazzo Valentini left me that way. A quick spoiler-free synopsis: it is the remains of Roman houses and a bathhouse discovered within the city in 2005. It uses projectors and lasers to map what aspects of the site looked like in the past based on the work of archaeologists and architects. Bringing the past to life purposefully is incredibly powerful when done well. I would never pretend that a school had the ability to do that but we can create those moments of awe and wonder while still retaining the rigour and validity of the discipline of history.

Why does the city stand out to me? It's a historic site that has had a role in so many historical events and periods associated in some way with primary history and beyond. It made me connect what I had learned and see it with more meaning.

I cannot say every history study has been joyous and life affirming. During my teaching degree, I studied several degree-level history units including patterns and periodisation (an overview of British history from ancient through to modern), Boudicca, Thermopylae and industrial Manchester ... however, I can't say that I loved every single unit of history. There were two semesters on Victorian agriculture during which time my love of the subject was tested. That's not to say I didn't learn from it but rather it stands out as not capturing my interest in the same way as the others. Because we have a national curriculum, we may have to face the challenge of teaching something that doesn't immediately capture our imagination. Finding the narrative that cuts through to children is a way I often use to make it mean something or captivate their attention. Independent schools, free schools and academies can choose to deviate as they wish of course.

When teaching, the aim has always been to share my passion and enthusiasm for the past with the children and teachers I work with. I think one of my favourite phrases in the current National Curriculum for history's Purpose of Study is: 'It should inspire pupils' curiosity to know more about the past.' After all, if we can capture a child's interest in a purposeful and meaningful way, that is a win. Those experiences and lessons have stayed with me since I was a child. I'll always see it as part of my role to pass that on. I know the idea of learning being defined as a change in the long-term memory is potentially controversial and limiting to some but the experiences I mentioned continue to stay with me and connect to what I encounter now so I'd like to think it has a role to play.

In effect, that's where the idea for this book came from – to consider which of the narratives of those rich experiences and opportunities we are telling and, more importantly, which we aren't.

2

WHAT IS PRIMARY HISTORY?

BEFORE WE START ...

- What would your definition for 'history' be?
- Have you ever thought about what influences the way in which you think about history?

Nothing like starting with a profound question ...

WHAT IS HISTORY?

If we look up the word history in the *Oxford English Dictionary*, the definition is:

> A written narrative constituting a continuous methodical record, in order of time, of important or public events, esp. those connected with a particular country, people, individual, etc.

> (OED, 1989)

Consider the breadth it covers: the importance of narratives and recording them with a methodology. If we take the Greek etymology of the word, *histor* and *historia*, it focuses on 'learned, wise man' and 'find out, narrative history'. This begins to explain that history is more than just the past itself but rather the process of finding out about the past.

Historian Greg Jenner makes a distinction between the past and history. He states: 'the past is what happened and cannot be changed' (Jenner, 2015), therefore we could argue it is objectively true and what actually happened. When explaining this, I use the concept of time travel in that, if it were possible, the past is what we would see unfold in front of us. However, history is different because it:

> is changing all the time. Is an intellectual discipline ... every generation rewrites its history. Every generation has different interests, things that they think are interesting and relevant. Things they want to know more about.

> (Jenner, 2015)

In history, it is challenging to think of something we say as objectively true beyond very simple snippets of information because ... well ... we weren't there and everyone that attempted to document what happened had their own perceptions of the world which inform who, what and how they documented the past! This is why you will often encounter the use of the word 'interpretation'. It is the nature of what historians do. In history, understanding is constructed by examining the available evidence base and interpreting it alongside what else is currently known and thought about that particular aspect of the past.

WHY DOES HISTORY CHANGE?

It is also vital to remember that there is not a complete documented account of any part of the the past. More than that though, even if a group of people had taken the time to produce such an impossibly weighty tome, a reader of history would need to ask many questions about who the authors were, their motivation for writing, particular beliefs and experiences which shaped their view of the world at that time. You may have heard of the phrase 'history is written by the victors' – which is invariably true when we think about which accounts survive from the past and how they present what took place. In 1961, Historian E.H. Carr wrote a book titled *What is History?* He wrote:

> when we attempt to answer the question 'What is History?' our answer, consciously or unconsciously, reflects our own position in time, and forms part of our answer to the broader question, what view we take of the society in which we live.
>
> (Carr, 1961, p. 3)

Carr compares the views of the world between the first edition of the *Cambridge Modern History*, edited by Lord John Dalberg-Acton in the late 1890s, and the second edition by Professor Sir George Clark in the 1950s. He writes:

> The clash between Acton and Sir George Clark is a reflection of the change in our total outlook on society over the interval between these two pronouncements. Acton speaks out of the positive belief, the clear-eyed self-confidence of the later Victorian age; Sir George Clark echoes the bewilderment and distracted scepticism of the beat generation.
>
> (Carr, 1961, p. 3)

What this reveals is that history is shaped by the world around the historian. In primary history, the changing shape of history is something to consider carefully in selecting what we should teach; it is as accurate a depiction as is possible given current understanding. The classic example is: did Vikings wear horned helmets into battle? Nope! But a favourite children's cartoon of the early 1990s and the Ladybird Book titled *Great Civilisations: The Vikings* (2014) both depicted them that way.

Our understanding of history changes because of new discoveries, new interpretations and new viewpoints.

> Take a minute to reflect on the last ten years; what shifts in emphasis for history teaching can you think of? Why did they happen? How have they shaped what, how and why you teach in certain ways?

If we reflect on the years 2020/21, there has been a clear shift in emphasis to the nature of which narratives we are choosing to teach in schools. Diversity, equality and decolonisation are hot topics for the curriculum in general. In history, there have been increasing calls to confront and acknowledge some of the more uncomfortable 'truths' about the United Kingdom's past in terms of empire and the role of different ethnic groups. This has not been met with universal positivity as some with a more traditional view of history have disagreed with this. This is explored more in Chapter 4.

WHAT DOES THIS MEAN FOR PRIMARY SCHOOL HISTORY?

Children's first interactions with history start far earlier than when they begin Key Stage 1. Before they start school, children will begin to encounter the past in the world around them: from walking past buildings like churches, watching TV, to conversations with older family members. Think about the stories you read to children or were read to you – how many were set in the past? All of this acts as an introduction.

Are they going to study it in the rigorous manner we would use in more formal history lessons? No, that would be incredibly difficult and go against the nature of EYFS pedagogy. Rather, when children encounter it they are provided with a start point from which curiosity can blossom as they enter more formally structured education.

This book focuses on history in Key Stage 1 and 2. However, it is important to acknowledge that children will have encountered aspects of the past as part of the EYFS curriculum and it forms part of the understanding the world early learning goal too. The different structure means that children encounter history alongside other subjects so part of the role of the Year 1 teacher is to continue to develop the children's understanding alongside a more formal introduction to the disciplinary side to the subject. In Chapter 3, the National Curriculum is the key focus so will not be mentioned in detail here.

The primary curriculum is different to secondary models. Not better or worse just different. The primary teacher can theoretically be responsible for 90 per cent of that pupil's education therefore the modes of delivery can vary when compared to a secondary model with separate departments working on their own piece of the puzzle. The overlap of disciplines and joy of a powerful connection is one of the reasons I love primary history. In a subject-discipline sense, this has meant that children studied a holistic topic but without an understanding of what primary history, geography etc. were.

PRIMARY HISTORY IN THE CLASSROOM

For the purposes of this book, I am drawing a distinction between a primary history lesson and a lesson which adds historical knowledge. In *Simplicitus* (2022), Emma Turner talks about the fact the primary curriculum is interconnected, which is absolutely the case across many schools. This is explained further in Chapter 12. Regardless of the pedagogical approach taken, certain key ideas are paramount to help children see history as being full of rich, varied and exciting narratives alongside a knowledge-base and skillset which enables them to understand, interpret and question those narratives they encounter.

1. **Children should encounter history and understand that history is a subject in its own right.** Specifically, this involves the development of substantive and disciplinary knowledge alongside the use of historically valid questions. This is why I have drawn a distinction between a history lesson and one which adds historical knowledge.

2. **Children should be actively taught that we do not have a complete picture of the past.** This is key to enable them to understand why certain questions cannot be answered, the process by which we learn about the past and why our understanding is ever-changing.

3. As the National Curriculum Purpose of Study states: '**inspire pupils' curiosity to find out more about the past**'. This is a primary teacher's bread and butter. It's important to ensure that this is not reduced to gimmicky lessons and cheap pops of enthusiasm which do not provide longlasting changes to understanding. I would like to think that we have moved beyond pretending that drawing, cutting out and painting a Roman shield is a history lesson.

4. A distinction between primary and secondary education is that **primary teachers often teach the class for 90 per cent of the week.** The outcome of this is that contextual understanding can be developed with careful and considered use of other curriculum subjects. Hinterland knowledge may be embedded via a different subject but part of the teacher's role is to curate and emphasise what is core knowledge which must be remembered.

WHY DOES PRIMARY HISTORY MATTER?

I have found no better way to explain this than the way Helen Carr and Suzannah Lipscomb described in their 2022 book *What is History, Now?*:

> My history was more than facts and dates; it was the feeling of the past, the myth, the magic, the stuff we didn't know. All of this was my way into history.
>
> (Carr and Lipscomb, 2021, p. 4)

Dates and facts matter but so does the role of curiosity ... so much so that it specifically states it in the Purpose of Study for the current national curriculum.

In the modern world, children have access to more information than at any point in the past. So why do children need to learn about the ancient world when they could just Google it? History doesn't provide children with a list of facts to know and remember. Hopefully, you are beginning to see it offers so much more than that. The factual knowledge is taught alongside disciplinary knowledge when children gain the understanding: of how knowledge has been acquired; the range of evidence that has been collated and interrogated; and the level of certainty of the current interpretation. Even at primary school, children can begin to understand what Carr wrote, that every historian expects 'their work to be superseded' (Carr, 1961, p. 3). Without this understanding of how our comprehension of the past is shaped, children could so easily struggle to make sense of how a meticulously constructed interpretation by a professional historian differs from what they may find on the internet. Access to information is a double-edged sword.

Primary history provides insight into where the world children live in began and starts the process of understanding how it has been shaped. By exploring narrative and discussing the rich narratives of the past, we can begin to illuminate the journey from humanity's earliest steps to civilisation and into the complex post-industrialised societies of the 20th century. As Christine Counsell wrote: 'The historical consciousness of children matters because they are human beings. History teaches us the meaning of human-ness' (cited in Culpin, 2007, p. 11). Personally, I like to describe history as helping children to begin to understand the story of humanity. When taught well, it helps them to make sense of what came before them and, in part, how the world they are growing up in was shaped.

To me, it matters because the many stories of the past have shaped today. We cannot ignore the legacies of those that came before us. We cannot pretend the past didn't happen. The story of human-ness is a complex, multifaceted messy assortment of fragmented understanding. If nothing else, the joy of primary history is that we are the first to support children to dip their toes into it.

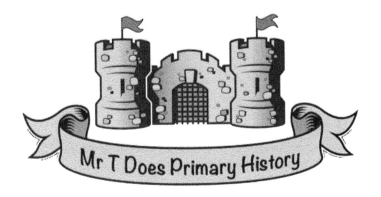

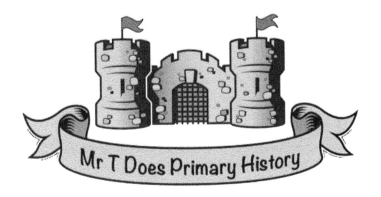Mr T Does Primary History

3

OPPORTUNITIES GRANTED IN THE NATIONAL CURRICULUM 2014 SPECIFICATION

BEFORE WE START ...

Be honest, have you taken the time to read the National Curriculum for History? Or, did you just look at the individual bullet point you happen to be teaching next? If the answer is the latter, can I suggest reading it before continuing with this chapter. The complete document offers more support than it may initially appear.

THE DEVELOPMENT OF HISTORY IN THE RECENT NATIONAL CURRICULUM

Pre-2014, history was taught differently in primary schools. The previous curriculum emphasised skills and provided supporting cross-curricular links. It set out what was to be taught in each key stage; there are notable differences in the emphasis provided compared to now. This was how I saw the curriculum when I was training – the more links the better in some cases ... even when they were tenuous beyond belief (more on this later). What we have today is a knowledge-rich approach influenced by the work of American educational theorist E.D. Hirsch (1988). This places a greater emphasis on the importance of the role of factual knowledge, with skills being secondary to what children know. Some would say skills are a type of procedural knowledge. However we define them, it's important to acknowledge that this has been a time of change both for what history we teach and how we teach it.

The current iteration of the National Curriculum (NC2014) was noticeably redrafted in 2013 after the original version to be released was criticised by many members of the teaching and historical community. The original iteration was a prescribed curriculum, proposing one long chronological narrative of British history and placing an enormous amount of content in Key Stage 2. The final redrafted version included world history and offered more flexibility in terms of who and what are taught. It retained many of the core principles which have further been developed. The vast majority of primary schools have spent immense amounts of time refining their curriculum offer after Ofsted inspections shifted their inspection emphasis in 2019.

When it was launched, Alf Wilkinson of the Historical Association stated in a DfE video from May 2014, 'the new history curriculum places much more emphasis on the big picture of history and chronological understanding of making sense of how it all fits together'. This was underpinned by Ofsted's previous history subject report titled *History for All* (2011). The role of chronology will be explored in Chapter 10 so I will just acknowledge that it is a concept embedded throughout the curriculum. Wilkinson goes on to say,

It's a framework. It's a series of headings. It's a series of content bullet points that gives teachers the opportunity to work within that to construct their own curriculum.

This framework structure is a double-edged sword. The DfE video goes on to say that a key challenge is to develop that coherent 'whole'. If you're a passionate lover of history with a clear vision, this is a joy to work within as there are so many avenues to explore and develop. However, primary teachers are not often subject specialists which means all those avenues that could be explored more cause fear around choosing the 'right' approach.

The purpose of this chapter is to explore the opportunities the framework structure grants us: to identify some ways in which the curriculum offer can be broad, diverse and representative. Finally, I will endeavour to highlight some common mistakes and misconceptions, including how to avoid them.

PURPOSE OF STUDY

This is the ultimate end point of the statutory curriculum and runs from Year 1 to Year 9. The intention here is to consider what our teaching will support the children to understand. It includes aspects of the discipline of history, the breadth of history to be encountered and understanding why studying history is both enjoyable and important. Every time we teach history, we are contributing to that as the final end point of the taught curriculum. On a personal level, the most important phrase is that: 'It should inspire pupils' curiosity to know more about the past' (DfE, 2013b). This is an important paragraph to read as a subject or curriculum lead – as a reminder to consider if the current curriculum provision facilitates this.

AIMS

There are six aims for history which focus on different aspects of what and how we teach history lessons. They begin with what the children should know, gain and understand, and add further clarity on the breadth of what is to be taught. While I do not advocate for these being referenced on medium-term plans, they should always play a role when we consider which aspects of the historical periods being taught are emphasised and connected to form the coherent picture of the past.

Christine Counsell wrote about the importance of core and hinterland knowledge in a blog: 'Even though clearly, as the word suggests, "hinterland" is just supporter or feeder of a core, when it comes to curriculum, the hinterland is as important as what is deemed core' (2018a, emphasis original). When making decisions about which knowledge to teach, it must be placed within the wider sense of time and place for it to be historicised knowledge. Aim 6 in particular provides clarity in the breadth of knowledge to be taught and the importance of making connections between what the children know and are learning now. To make the most of the opportunities offered by the NC2014, it's important that those responsible for planning and implementing it look at the document as a whole and not something to choose isolated extracts from.

Table 3.1   Brief summary of each aim

1	The important role chronology plays across the curriculum. This includes the emphasis on the chronological narrative of British history and aspects which have influenced Britain and the wider world today.
2	The breadth of world history be encountered. Focusing on the ways of life, achievements and mistakes that have been made.
3	Teaching abstract substantive concepts which may be confused with the importance of vocabulary lists. A historically grounded understanding is rooted in the context of specific periods of time.
4	History as a discipline including core disciplinary concepts and their purpose within the subject.
5	The process of historical enquiry as a vehicle to introduce how the past is studied by historians.
6	The breadth of the curriculum and making connections across what has been learned. Connections are focused around locality (Chapter 5); branches of history such as social military etc. and over differing timescales.

ATTAINMENT TARGETS

The one sentence we are given on attainment in the curriculum initially looks less than helpful. However, it ties into the knowledge-rich curriculum approach and reminds us that the children need to know, make use of and understand what they have been taught. Therefore, knowing more, remembering more is an important concept when we think about both what and how we teach. In terms of opportunities, the key is that the information is from the school's programme of study – the opportunities we can make the most of. You may have heard of the phrase 'the curriculum is the progression model'; Michael Fordham describes it as the journey children go on in order to get better at the subject. Attainment, like the curriculum offer, is school-specific.

SUBJECT CONTENT

When reflecting on what is taught at your school, consider:

- have you kept in the classics because they have always been taught?
- how does your curriculum reflect your children's context and demographics?
- is the provision broad and ambitious or just meeting the minimum outline spec?

This contains two sections that work together to combine the processes and specific content children are going to encounter as they proceed through the curriculum. The processes could so easily be described as skills, and often are, in school progression documents, but this term can become muddy when we think about concepts. For the sake of ease, the term 'processes' defines them accurately enough. These should be embedded across every unit of history to be taught and used in conjunction with the specific bullet point content. The specific bullet points need only be encountered once but should be linked to comparable knowledge studied subsequently.

In 2014, Jamie Byrom produced a document for the Historical Association focusing on progression in history under the then new curriculum. He wrote:

isolated 'coverage' of these areas of study and the exemplars provided under them will not, on its own, develop the sort of knowledge that is needed. It is not enough for pupils to work their way through the listed material even if they experience highly enjoyable activities and display good levels of knowledge and understanding of the work put before them: something bigger has to happen.

(Byrom, 2014, p. 3)

This is key when we consider the framework that Wilkinson spoke about (DfE, 2014). The knowledge must be connected, as aim 6 states. This is spoken of in terms of strengthening the child's schema of a concept in their mind – something we will explore further in Chapter 6. Figure 3.1 shows how Byrom exemplified the difference between the two types of subject content.

KEY STAGE 1

The bullet points detail specific content to be taught. In Key Stage 1, there is immense flexibility to meet the curriculum specification as it talks about changes within living memory, events beyond living memory etc. While suggestions are given on which could be chosen, the flexibility offers schools the chance to tailor their choices to their school's particular cohorts and context.

WHAT DOES LIVING MEMORY MEAN?

A common misconception is that 'within living memory' means the child's own memory in Key Stage 1. This is not the case. It refers to the last century and the concept that we could theoretically speak to a person that was there about it. The child's own living memory is a start point for chronology in the early years stage.

SIGNIFICANT INDIVIDUALS

The concept of significance in a historical sense is complex and nuanced (isn't everything related to this subject!). In Key Stage 1, children can be introduced to the concept of something being

Key Stage 1

Knowledge / understanding of British history	*Knowledge/understanding of wider world history*	*The ability/disposition to:*
☐ Changes within living memory – used, where appropriate, to reveal changes in national life See also wider world history	☐ Events from beyond living memory that are significant nationally or globally	☐ Be aware of the past, using common words & phrases relating to time
	☐ Lives of significant individuals in the past who have contributed to national and international achievements. Some should be used to compare aspects of life in different periods	☐ Fit people/events into chronological framework
Local history		☐ Identify similarities/differences between periods
☐ Significant historical events, people and places in their own locality		☐ Use wide vocabulary of everyday historical terms
		☐ Ask and answer questions
		☐ Choose and use from stories and other sources to show understanding
		☐ Understand some ways we find out about the past
		☐ Identify different ways in which past is represented

(Continued)

Figure 3.1 (Continued)

Key Stage 2

The following areas of study taught through a combination of overview and depth studies

Knowledge/understanding of British history	*Knowledge/understanding of wider world history*	*The ability/disposition to:*
☐ Changes in Britain from the Stone Age to the Iron Age	☐ The achievements of the earliest civilisations; depth study of one of: • Sumer • Indus Valley • Egypt • Shang Dynasty	☐ Continue to develop chronologically secure knowledge of history
☐ The Roman Empire and its impact on Britain		☐ Establish clear narratives within and across periods studied
☐ Britain's settlement by Anglo-Saxons and Scots		☐ Note connections, contrasts and trends over time
☐ Viking and Anglo-Saxon struggle for the kingdom of England to the time of Edward the Confessor	☐ Ancient Greece – life, achievements, influence	☐ Develop the appropriate use of historical terms
☐ An aspect or theme of British history that extends pupils' chronological knowledge beyond 1066	☐ Non-European society that contrasts with British history. One of: • early Islamic civilisations inc study of Baghdad c. 900AD • Mayan civilisation c. 900AD • Benin (west Africa) c. 900-1300	☐ Regularly address and sometimes devise historically valid questions
Local history		☐ Understand how knowledge of the past is constructed from a range of sources
• A local study		☐ Construct informed responses by selecting and organizing relevant historical information
		☐ Understand that different versions of the past may exist, giving some reasons for this (Not explicitly stated but is natural progression between KS1 and KS3

Figure 3.1 National curriculum history: aspects to develop (Byrom, 2014)

Note: Copyright: this is included with kind permission from Jamie Byrom and the Historical Association. The full document is available from the Historical Association: https://www.history.org.uk/primary/resource/7879/progression-from-eyfs-to-key-stage-3 (accessed 16 November 2022).

significant as being worthy of remembrance for either positive or negative reasons. This is different to being 'famous' and the two should not be confused as it can create misconceptions about fame being a determiner for significance. Also, in the 21st century, this is problematic as there are many people in the public eye because ... they are in the public eye – instead of for what they accomplished, discovered etc. In addition, a person's relative significance may not have been realised during their lifetime, only posthumously – such as Victorian palaeontologist Mary Anning, who recently had a statue of her unveiled in her home town of Lyme Regis after a campaign led by a child. Finally, if something was described as significant at one point, it does not mean that is guaranteed throughout time as perceptions can and do change. This is about how we look at explorers such as Columbus and Cook. Their impact on Indigenous populations is something that is important to take account of.

LOCALITY

Local history is on everyone's doorstep by its very nature. However, if teachers jump for the most notable landmarks, the lesser-known gems can be missed and children may wrongly assume that there is no history on their doorsteps. When thinking about teaching local history, think about ripples in a pond. Start very close in EYFS by thinking about changes within the school building itself; it is all abstract to them even though it may seem obvious to adults. Has there been building work which makes the building markedly different? Can children speak to parents and grandparents that previously attended? In Key Stage 1, step outwards to look around the village or town at most; changes in the high street using photographs through time or the church as a source of evidence and how its role has endured since it was built. When the children reach Key Stage 2, this can be expanded outwards once again as part of a more coherent and in-depth understanding. If there was a notable individual this can, of course, be taught; but remember, local history can be right on your doorstep. This is explored further in Chapter 5.

COMMON MISTAKES AND OPPORTUNITIES

There is no singular way in which the curriculum must be delivered. There is no 'correct' way in which it should be delivered. This means teachers can make the most of the flexibility within it. What matters is careful consideration of what is taught and why it was selected. The locality example above is one approach by which this can be exploited to create a bespoke curriculum highlighting what one school places importance on.

When teaching significant individuals, it is easy to retain the classic choices of Florence Nightingale, Columbus et al. But this misses an opportunity to add rich and varied stories the children may not otherwise encounter. It introduces them to cultures that may be the heritage of families in the school community while highlighting the achievements of other groups. If you are teaching about the race to the pole, think about talking about Matthew Henson, an African American, who was a member of a successful expedition that claimed to have reached the geographic North Pole in 1909. If you are studying the exploration of Europeans such as Columbus and Cook, consider pairing them with someone like Ibn Battuta, a Moroccan-born explorer who journeyed circa 75,000 miles in the 14th century. It took him across Africa, the Middle East, India and elsewhere in Europe.

Easily missed within this objective is the phrase 'Some should be used to compare aspects of life in different periods' (DfE, 2013b), which means at least once, the children must study a pair of individuals from different time periods to study how life differed through time.

Local history doesn't have to be kept as a single stand-alone unit of work either, although I would always advocate for at least one of these units per key stage. Teaching the Great Fire of London (1666) is still incredibly popular in schools but there were other fires across the country. When working with schools in Bradford, we have added a small additional enquiry which uses a local example of the Bradford City FC fire (1985) as a vehicle by which to study changes in technology used for firefighting. This is further explored in Chapter 5. There are many other examples out there.

KEY STAGE 2

Although Key Stage 2 is more prescribed, it is still those broad-brush strokes that Alf Wilkinson spoke about when the curriculum was launched (DfE, 2014). Changes in Britain from the Stone Age to Iron Age ... Which changes? How do we think about those changes? The post-1066 study offers immense possibilities to tailor the curriculum to a school's context, demographics and locality. More than that, nothing in the document restricts you to those episodes in history so teachers can exceed the specification should they have sufficient capacity. If this is done, consider the opportunity cost of having more history to cover at the expense of spending more time on what must be taught – do children have sufficient time to really gain a depth of understanding?

A number of the objectives in this key stage are multi-part and can often require several enquiries to cover all of it. While they do not need to be covered in equal depth, they are all relevant and often lead naturally from one into another. In the worked examples on the Romans, this is the approach taken. Table 3.2 contains the units where this is required and Figure 3.2 shows where I take that approach to enable sufficient breadth to be covered.

Table 3.2   Multi-part objectives

Period taught	Emphasis 1	Emphasis 2
Romans	The Roman Empire	The impact it had on Britain
Earliest civilisations	Overview of all civilisations	One of them in depth
Ancient Greece	A study of Greek life and achievements	Their influence on the Western world

The most common mistake I have encountered in primary history is the requirement to teach an overview of where and when the first civilisations emerged. It is specified and can be studied before or after the in-depth study but must be studied.

I choose to break some objectives because of what it enables me to teach. However, this is a choice I make and not a requirement. This can be seen below in Figure 3.2.

Anglo-Saxon and Viking conflict	Challenging a stereotypical view of the Vikings	The conflict for the kingdom of England, focusing on Alfred and his descendants
The Vikings have an enduring reputation as vicious raiders through time which has been depicted multiple times in film, television etc. The first enquiry studies them through that lens but also their other accomplishments in trade and exploration. The purpose is to challenge that singular interpretation and consider from whose perspective it may have arisen.		
The second enquiry focuses specifically on the NC objective and the struggle for the Kingdom of England. I choose to focus on Alfred as he is the only English king to warrant the title of 'the Great' around his actions and subsequent unification through his children and grandson.		
Non-European study	The nature of life and the achievements of the civilisation	A comparison with Britain at that time
The Non-European study (Benin, Maya or Early Islamic) has become my favourite to learn about because I knew very little of them before it was added to the curriculum. They offer the chance for children to study the history of a different part of the world in a positive context. Given this, the first enquiry introduces the children to life and the achievements of these civilisations.		
The second enquiry functions as a retrieval exercise but wider comparison that life was hugely varied at different locations across the globe even when timelines are concurrent. In the early medieval period, it could be argued that Britain was not so 'great' compared to elsewhere. NB: Great Britain did not exist until much later.		

Figure 3.2 Units that I *choose* to break into multiple parts. Under each emphasis is a brief explanation of why this approach is taken. The post-1066 study could fit into this model depending on what was selected

CONTENT NOT LISTED

Some popular units from national curricula gone by were not included for primary during this curriculum reform. A number are in the programme of study for Key Stage 3 such as the Tudors or the Second World War. Does this mean they can't be taught as part of the primary curriculum? Absolutely not! They can be included as the curriculum sets out the minimum standard to be met rather than an aspirational ambition. If this is something that your school does, take some time to ensure you aren't merely ensuring children are taught the same content twice at different stages at education ... there is more than enough history to go around.

SUMMARY

The curriculum structure offers flexibility when we have the time to read, research and consider what would be most powerful for our children to know and understand. In addition, academies and free schools do not have to teach the NC as published so this offers the chance for a truly broad and ambitious curriculum.

One thing to consider before having the child in a sweet shop moment: does adding mountains of extra content make for a better curriculum? To me, no; it's a case of balance.

Why that? Why now? Do we need to condense the rest of the curriculum so much to ensure Year 6 can teach both world wars over two terms?

'Opportunity cost' is a phrase to consider here: what benefits are granted by adding additional content vs the opportunities lost to really understand what children must be taught at this age? When thinking about the curriculum sequencing and structure, this thought is something I keep front and centre.

The final two chapters in this book give two worked examples that exemplify the planning sequence I use. Within them, I will be referencing each area of the NC document and how it helped to shape the decisions I made over which aspects to teach. The intention is that it will help exemplify what I'm attempting to accomplish in each unit of work and the coherence I'd build across the curriculum as a whole.

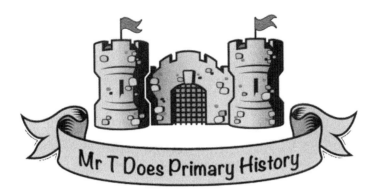

4

WHOSE NARRATIVE ARE WE TEACHING?

Take a look at the curriculum you are currently teaching:

- To what extent would you say it is diverse and representative?
- Is this a recent change and what was the catalyst for this?

Make a list of which diverse voices you are teaching and the value they add to your curriculum offer.

HISTORY IS REWRITTEN

As said by historian Greg Jenner, history is rewritten by each generation (2015). I would be surprised if many schools had not looked at
their curriculum in light of recent events such as the murder of
George Floyd in the US and the toppling of Edward Colston's statue
in Bristol in June 2020. There has been a level of political debate and
argument over the concept of free speech linked to decolonising the
curriculum, including comments made by former universities minister Michelle Donelan, who said, in a *Daily Telegraph* podcast in
February 2021:

> The so-called decolonisation of the curriculum, is in effect, cen-
> soring history. As a history student, I'm a vehement protector and
> champion of safeguarding our history. It otherwise becomes fic-
> tion, if you start editing it, taking bits out that we view as stains.

In primary history, many schools have taken the opportunity to rei-
magine what is taught at their school and why those choices were
made. This shift in emphasis has been viewed by some as a political
move in the current climate of culture wars, 'wokeness' and populist
views on left and right.

More widely, there has been a multitude of projects, books and
more that consider the diverse nature of the past and connections to
controversial histories that have gone unrealised or, at least, been
under-represented. Some of these will be mentioned in this chapter
but I would encourage teachers to consider the title of this chapter
carefully ... whose narratives are we teaching? More importantly,
whose narratives aren't we teaching and why?

WHAT IS A DIVERSE CURRICULUM?

Diversity is by its very nature multifaceted. There are so many possible ways we could divide the past in an attempt to consider how
varied stories could be represented. The 2019 *Summer Resource* from
the Historical Association said:

> We believe that diversity needs to be broadly defined and include different ethnic communities, genders, classes, together with other facets of diversity such as localities, religious perspectives, disability, etc.

which highlights the range of voices that can contribute to the children's growing understanding of the past. It could also create a daunting list of voices we must listen to at every opportunity which could so easily be reduced to an over-simplified tokenistic gesture.

It is almost impossible to include every diverse voice in the same manner and with the same weighting across the history curriculum for reasons including the range of evidence to support understanding and the role it played within that particular event or period of history. When we use focused enquiry questions (see Chapter 11), this becomes an easier prospect because the diverse stories we choose to tell, like all stories, must add value to that enquiry. Focusing on what the children will know enables teachers to think carefully about what is taught and how those varied voices contribute to that clearly defined emphasis. Within the two worked examples at the end of the book, a range of voices is heard, adding breadth but, more importantly, value.

POLITICALLY VOLATILE OR CONTROVERSIAL HISTORIES

Placing the quote from the former university minister in the first paragraph was entirely deliberate within this chapter. There are many viewpoints from which people consider the past which is why history is full of debate and argument. As part of this book, I am endeavouring not to come down on any particular side of the metaphorical fence but rather open up thought processes. It would be wonderful to say that diversifying the curriculum could be done in a politically neutral manner without any 'side' of the aisle (in a political sense) taking offence or objection to it. Sadly, this hasn't been the case and, if I'm honest, is unlikely to ever be possible. One of the joys of the current curriculum is that there is a framework we must meet but it can be tailored to our individual school's context as mentioned in the previous chapter.

The National Trust's report into colonialism and historic slavery was released in September 2020 (National Trust, 2020b). In the publication announcement, it said:

> Data in the report includes the historic sources of wealth linked to the global slave trades, goods and products of enslaved labour and the East India Company for significant buildings and estates in our care. It also documents the historic houses linked to the abolition of slavery and campaigns against colonial oppression.

This would appear to be an attempt to make valid historical links to the way in which the wealth was brought into Britain as its empire expanded in line with aim 2 of the curriculum. This is important because contextualising the past is a good way to express the manner in which people lived on a societal level. It is also the nature of what historians do. As Carr wrote in *What is History?*, historians expect their work to be superseded again and again (1961).

This is one example of viewing the past with a changed perspective. Sometimes history is studied through a critical lens in an attempt to stop injustices happening again. Because of this, history cannot be presented as a balance sheet: this aspect is abhorrent but they weren't all bad because of ... The changing interpretations will create differing responses with those of specific beliefs and viewpoints. The response to this report by branches of the media are easy to find and offer an alternate perspective to the author's stated intentions. History isn't an agreed list of facts; it is ever-changing understanding and consideration.

When teaching young children, it's vital to pay close attention to the nature of what is going to be taught.

Two questions to consider:

- is the content appropriate for children of that age?
- will it be taught by specialist teachers in secondary?

It is absolutely possible to teach a diverse curriculum without veering towards controversy at every step. Children can learn through a purposeful curriculum that tells a range of stories which add value and breadth, using a combination of positive role models and the unpleasant features of the past.

WHY DOES IT MATTER?

Anecdotally, one of the most joyous moments in my teaching career came when I was teaching a Year 6 class about aspects of the First World War during the centenary years of 2014–18. The class included children from a range of heritages and, to begin with, I had kept to what I learned in secondary history lessons. The classics were covered such as the two European power blocks growing in the early 20th century, Gavrilo Princip shooting Archduke Franz Ferdinand and the local Leeds Pals battalion's role. But then, my perspective was shifted by Andrew Wrenn's presentation during a Yorkshire History Forum and 2018 article titled 'For whose God, King and country? Seeing the First World War through South Asian eyes' (2018), which highlighted a glaring omission on my part because I simply was not aware and had never been taught in this area. India had been part of the Empire since the 18th century and Britain therefore called upon soldiers from across its empire. Children whose families migrated over from India saw themselves represented in what they were learning about. The moments of 'he looks like me' brought history to life for them and in no way, shape or form took away from the white British children. That was a turning point in my thinking. There was also a powerful local connection which will be explained further in the next chapter. All I did was add another voice to the story that I was telling. The Indian army fighting on the battlefields in the same manner as the Canadian troops on Vancouver corner.

A really thought-provoking analogy for this also came from Steve Adcock's blog from June 2021 titled 'Curriculum: The mirror and the window' (2021). In it, he wrote about this beautiful metaphor for why diversity matters:

The mirror signifying that all pupils would see themselves in our curriculum. The window representing our ambition to show all pupils the world beyond their immediate experience. And so it was that our work to enrich our curriculum to better reflect the diversity of our country became less about balancing different perspectives, and more about bringing all pupils into a shared story.

To that end, where a school community is a very stable white working-class mining community, the window is key to broaden children's horizons beyond their immediate locality and experiences. When it's an incredibly diverse community that may have changed in recent years, the mirror shines to introduce children to not only the past they can relate to but that of their peers and beyond. In Key Stage 1, there is immense opportunity to accomplish this because of how open the subject content is. In Key Stage 2, focus carefully on which ancient civilisation is studied in depth and why, which non-European study and why, and which post-1066 study ... and why? Find a meaningful curriculum for your school community.

THE CURRICULUM I LEARNED

In a 2016 video titled *Slavery and the Cotton Mills* (BBC, 2016), historian David Olusoga said:

> When I was growing up in the North of England, this is what I was taught at school. The history of the Industrial Revolution and I was told that this was my history because it was the heritage of the white working-class side of my family. But I was never told, not once, that the cotton that made places like this so incredibly profitable was produced by slaves 3,000 miles away in the deep South. The black slaves of America never set foot on British soil but are part of British history.

As a child growing up in the 1990s in the North of England, I remember learning about the slave trade in Year 8 and being appalled at the treatment of people being bought and sold as property. I was also taught about the immense riches brought to Yorkshire because of the Industrial Revolution through the mills in Armley. What I wasn't taught was the connection between the two, which would have linked these two facets of my understanding together. It could have presented a more coherent narrative.

The women I encountered in primary history that spring to mind were the 'classics' as we would perhaps now call them: Florence Nightingale, Queen Victoria, Boudicca and the six wives of Henry VIII. There may have been others that I have forgotten but they don't reflect the diversity of women's experience and their impact on history, do they? If the only women children learn about in the curriculum are nurses and queens, it doesn't provide the breadth of aspirational role models that inspire children to pronounce 'I want to be like them', does it? These are two examples that jump to mind. There are many others, of course; but which narratives would enhance your children's understanding of the past in a meaningful manner? That is a question that can be revisited again and again.

HISTORY IS MADE OF NARRATIVES … AVOIDING TOKEN GESTURES

As discussed in Chapter 2, the etymology of history emphasises the important role of narratives within the subject. When diversifying the curriculum content, it's important that the changes are carefully considered and enhance the children's understanding instead of being a bolt-on gesture.

Black history month in the UK takes place each October and many schools embrace it as a chance to mark more diverse histories. However, the opportunity is lessened if this is the only example through the year. There are many other months through the year (see Table 4.1) that can provide this link. Also, think carefully about which narratives are taught and the implication of those that are not taught. Popular choices include the lives of Rosa Parks, Ruby Bridges and Nelson Mandela; what don't these important stories include? The simple answer is that, by omission, it looks like discrimination didn't occur in the UK – which is wrong. A powerful example is to ensure children learning about Rosa Parks also understand the story of the Bristol bus boycott. The two stories are not exact copies, but they have a common thread which highlights that discrimination was encountered in Britain as well as the US during the 20th century. It also leads to the idea that black history only recently came to be part of British history which is, once again, untrue. Within the Roman unit, there are three pertinent examples of black history told within as part of the wider sense of time and place.

Table 4.1 gives a list of months that can be marked through the year. Not all of them need to carry the same weighting in terms of curriculum time but they are all powerful opportunities to tell different stories in an assembly, a class book in English or a significant individual in history. If you choose to miss out one or more of them in full, consider why and what value it could offer.

Table 4.1   History-related days and months through the school year

Month	Emphasis
October	Black history month
11 November	Remembrance day
18 November to 18 December	Disability history month
February	LGBT history month
May	Local history month
March	Women's history month
27 January	Holocaust memorial day
20 June	World refugee day
22 June	Windrush day

In their book *What is History, Now?* authors Carr and Lipscomb write that the contributors:

address marginalised histories that were not part of the mainstream narrative in 1961 (when *What is History?* was published): the history of women, Black history, queer histories, the history of people with disabilities and Indigenous histories.

(2021, p. 16)

Since this point, Britain has developed into a multicultural, tolerant democratic society where all should be treated and viewed as equals under the eyes of the law. The law has changed so, surely, it's right and proper the historical narratives we teach reflect this too.

SUMMARY

Consider which of these dates and months are taught at your school. Specifically, drill down into the detail of who, what and how they are taught. What impression does this leave with children and is it as rounded a knowledge base as possible? When considering the curriculum as a whole, this is a good place to start, reflect and continue to develop.

5

THE IMPORTANCE OF LOCALITY

BEFORE WE START ...

Think about what you would regard as local history and why. Now, compare this with what your school teaches and calls a 'local' study.

WHAT IS LOCAL HISTORY?

In the current iteration of the National Curriculum, there is no spec-ification as to what local actually means. When asked, I will often flippantly quote a distance of around 4.6 miles with a smirk on my face. Hales (2018, p. 673) wrote:

> Coming to a consensus of what local history is and what local history study entails, is somewhat problematic. Historians themselves vary in their appreciation and definitions of local history. Distinct areas, such as those where there are with well-known historical heritage sites or which are significant in national or global events (high-status history) are often high-lighted in the media, studied and written about by historians. This gives the impression that local history is about areas with high-status history; others see local history as being more about the lives of ordinary people within an area, regardless of their economic or social status and the contribution they have made to that area (Claire 1996; Jackson 2008; Wood 2012; Dixon and Hales 2014).

This presents a difficulty in terms of what actually counts as a 'local' study?

My preferred metaphor here is to think about ripples in a pond. By this I mean, every time the children study local history, it can be taken one step outwards. If there is a powerful example from your locality that ties into the wider history curriculum, that is a purposeful addi-tion to incorporate within that unit of work. However, local history can stand on its own merit. It is an introduction to how the past is still around us today, the changing shape and 'face' of the children's immediate environment ... sometimes telling the stories of people that lived on the doorstep is that eye-opening moment. Children can walk in the footsteps of those that came before. Children can have their eyes opened to how the world around them was shaped. It doesn't have to be high-status history; it can be the lives of the ordi-nary folk. That is one of the joys of local history for me.

HOW LOCAL IS IT?

The first step to think about is how local is it? Even though there is no definition in the curriculum of what locality means, stepping beyond the village or town in EYFS and Key Stage 1 means things can so easily be missed. History is full of abstract worlds and lives, which is why Chapter 8 introduces the important role of world-building in contextualising the past. For local history, this is so much easier because we can get out and about to see it.

> Think about what could be reached within a ten-minute walk of your school. What stories do they tell and how has their role or use changed over time?

My favoured start points:

- the school building itself
- buildings along the streets around the school
- the park
- the church.

While training, I was lucky enough to be have the brilliant Beverley Forrest as my history tutor. She instilled not only the merits of teaching history but the sheer joy that could be found by connecting what was around me in meaningful ways. Her influence shapes both what I consider teaching as a local study and how it is delivered. Bev has written on the subject for many publications and, if further support or inspiration is needed, these should be high on the list of reference points.

When teaching, go and visit these local sites. Visit them more than once to use and apply the children's growing knowledge base. They can arrive with a new and different question which continuously adds value and reduces the chance of learning becoming stale. Think, how many times children have played in the park without realising where it came from (it was a gift to the town from the local mill owner). Its name derives from a family of local significance. That bandstand they hide in while it's raining has been the site of one for over a hundred years ... would you like to see the photos of it? This is why local history is brilliant! The other advantage, with more recent local history, is there are community members that can offer personal experience and testimony of events. This is always a rich opportunity because it brings the past to life with a range of perspectives, viewpoints and emotive experiences – storytelling is a powerful tool.

RIPPLING OUTWARDS

There is a minimum requirement to teach two local history units in primary history. In Chapter 3 the flexibility and opportunities contained within this curriculum were explored. This is also a factor when thinking about how locality can be a key feature in a history curriculum.

Some things to consider:

1. **Does every local study need to cover a half-term?** No, they can vary hugely and be tied into different sites and events throughout the year. Some may be blocked into a focus week and others can run longer.
2. **Can we teach about a significant individual and then look at their impact more widely later in the curriculum**? Yes, absolutely. This is what I mean by rippling outwards and the local example I have taught at a school in Leeds; it is included in Table 5.1.
3. **There is no local history near to me; the nearest site is in the city centre (an hour away).** I would be surprised if this is true. It may take a bit of digging around but there will be brilliant stories nearby ... it's a case of knowing where to look and who to ask. There are some suggestions in Table 5.1.

Table 5.1 A local approach taken for a Leeds school. They vary in depth and are embedded when relevant. They sit alongside relevant opportunities for geography fieldwork on human geography. Locality is also embedded throughout the British history units as and where it adds value

EYFS	KS1	LKS2	UKS2
How their immediate locality changes through the year	A study of the local park and who it is named after	Why was the canal dug in our locality?	Why did Leeds thrive during the Industrial Revolution?
Did the school look different in the past?	What can the church tell us about life in the past?		Who is commemorated on our local memorial?

TEACHING A LOCAL STUDY

In essence, a local history study will be structured in a similar manner to the one advocated for in this book – led by focused historical enquiry questions (see Chapter 11 for more detail) and making use of a range of source materials to construct an evidence-led answer by the end of it. However, there are elements of local studies which are different for important reasons.

A local study requires a specific focus on the locality which means finding a generic product off the shelf is unlikely to be possible. This also means that looking for support and resources needs to be done proactively and earlier than for other units of work. There are many places to begin the search:

- library
- museums
- archives
- community groups
- British Association of Local History branches
- Historical Association branches.

Before attempting to fully decide upon the lesson sequence and overall enquiry questions, take some time to review the evidence base that is available. This means that it is easier to understand what possible outcomes there are and therefore pose specific questions to lead towards them. It also allows the teacher to ascertain what they are yet to find and therefore refine requests from other potential leads and sources.

Finally, where appropriate relate local stories to national or global narratives. This ensures children can see history as more than just isolated episodes. Hales (2018) identified this as a deficiency of the QCA schemes of work that were used in the early 2000s. If we think back to the chapter on understanding the National Curriculum, aim 6 specifies the important role of connecting children's growing knowledge base. Look back at the local example in Table 5.1. There is a deliberate narrative taught across those local study examples which progressively introduces children to the concept of the Industrial Revolution. In upper Key Stage 2, this local study is then compared outwards to look at how this was different to other parts of the country.

Although local studies should stand on their own merit, they can be embedded across the curriculum in many ways to once again connect the local stories into wider narratives. They provide a way for children to see the past being all around them and not just happening elsewhere.

Examples I have used in the past:

- Jogendra Sen and the Leeds Pals
- Roman York as an introduction to locality
- comparing the Great Fire of London to a pertinent local example
- which kingdom were the children in during British history.

THE IMPORTANCE OF PLACE AND LOCATION

Studying local history can act as a brilliant vehicle by which to embed purposeful interdisciplinary links. In particular, geography fieldwork as collection of suitable data is a useful activity in both subjects. Ofsted wrote about geography fieldwork in primary schools:

Fieldwork is vital to geographical practice, but this was weak in key stage 2 in many of the schools we inspected. That's not to say that pupils did not visit different places, but, when they did, they did not make the observations or collect data that they could analyse and present their findings. Fieldwork was much stronger in the early years and key stage 1.

(Ofsted, 2021c)

This is an opportunity missed as the data collection can be used to inform a local history study focusing on current building occupation on the high street compared to that in the past or the purpose of the canals today compared to when they were first constructed. Both disciplines involve the impact humanity have had on the surroundings. Both can help children to have a better understanding of their immediate locality.

SUMMARY

Think carefully about your local examples once again. Can you embed locality as a substantive part of wider historical studies? What value do your current local studies offer? Can they be combined with other important subject disciplines?

1. How local are your local studies? Where possible, carefully blend high-status history with those beautiful stories of how your immediate locality has developed over time and been shaped.

2. Are you connecting local and national pictures? While not always possible or viable given limited curriculum time, consider how teaching the children about local examples, such as prehistoric monuments or Roman settlements, could both inspire curiosity (to which the purpose of study rightly gives importance) and add meaningful evidence to the children's developing understanding of the past.

3. Does it offer purposeful cross-curricular links? Once again, this is not always possible or viable but can provide rich opportunities to highlight the powerful crossover between the humanities and beyond.

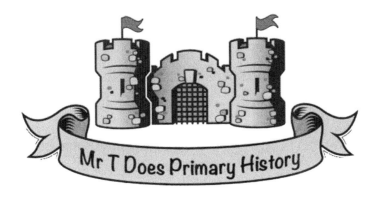

6

CONSIDERATIONS WHEN STARTING TO PLAN A UNIT OF WORK

BEFORE WE START ...

- Which pieces of research have changed the way you work in the classroom?
- Did you adopt them wholesale or cherry pick what worked for your setting?

While I will be providing a brief introduction to the research in question, it will be in the specific context of how it impacts the way I approach history curriculum thinking and teaching in the classroom. As I wrote at the outset, the research will focus in on this specific purpose; I would encourage you to read the examples in full to gain a deeper understanding.

RESEARCH AND EVIDENCE HAVE AN IMPORTANT ROLE IN BOTH WHAT WE TEACH AND THE WAY IN WHICH IT IS TAUGHT

Thinking back to my own teacher training, I was introduced to certain pieces of academic research that underpinned educational thinking, some of which has been debunked and some of which still carries important weight in my teaching practice. If you were teaching in the early 2000s, learning styles were all the rage. How we catered for visual, auditory and kinaesthetic learners was referenced on lesson plans to ensure their preferred style was accommodated. Fast forward to the 2020s and learning styles have pretty much gone the way of the dinosaurs. Chapter 3 discusses the changes brought to the curriculum in 2014 as influenced by the work of American academic E. D Hirsch. Therefore, whether at a national policy level or in one's own classroom, academic research has a clear influence.

Formative assessment from Black and Wiliam's *Inside the Black Box Raising Standards Through Classroom Assessment* (2005, originally published 1998) still plays an important role in how I teach and the way in which I put units of work together. Formative assessment helps to ensure that children understand what they have been taught and allows intervention during lessons to address misconceptions immediately. This, alongside the work of Bill Rogers on behaviour management and Shirley Clarke on feedback, shaped the way my classroom work still looks today. Why bring this up? Research and evidence have an important role in both what we teach and the way in which it is taught. It continues to inform my own beliefs around education and changes the way I view teaching as a profession.

Something I've realised over time is the importance of listening to opposing viewpoints. More importantly, be willing to change your mind on something. In the world of social media, intransigent positions have become the norm and 280 characters is how a complex, nuanced position can be set out. The devil is ALWAYS in the detail. Whenever we encounter academic research, a new pedagogical approach etc., think carefully: how can I make this work for me? What does this offer that adds to what I do now?

COGNITIVE SCIENCE AND MEMORY

There has been growth in the influence of cognitive science on schools over the past few years. Books such as Daniel Willingham's *Why Don't Students Like School?* (2009) have informed schools and teachers on how to consider the way in which the mind thinks, works and remembers what has been encountered and, specifically, the significant role of story in learning which is perfectly in line with history as a narrative subject. In addition, Chapter 3 (Willingham, 2021) focuses on getting students to remember what is learned, citing the important role of creating meaning as an influence on both the chances of learning being remembered and also the way in which it is remembered.

The concept of cognitive load theory, as proposed by Sweller in 1988, is an important consideration as to how we segment units of work but also individual lessons. When, in January 2017, Dylan Wiliam pronounced on Twitter that cognitive load theory was 'the single most important thing for teachers to know', it made me and many others sit up and pay attention. Oliver Lovell writes, in his book on this theory:

> because the environment is effectively limitless in scope, and our long-term memory is effectively limitless in its capacity, working memory – the only *limited* component of our memory system – acts as a bottleneck.
>
> (2020, pp. 19–20, emphasis in original)

Ofsted wrote about cognitive load theory in a 2019 article that explained short-term and long-term memory as being made up of a range of schemata. This is key as to why we need to think carefully about how we present new knowledge to children and the way in which we navigate through the taught curriculum. Too much, too soon and in an overly complex way is likely to lead to cognitive overload and not learning. Alongside this, when making links between prior learning and new learning, it's important to create and strengthen connections to support children's developing understanding.

In addition, the way in which lessons are delivered is now under-pinned by the work of people like Rosenshine, using his principles of instruction:

> These principles come from three sources: (a) research in cognitive science, (b) research on master teachers, and (c) research on cognitive supports.
>
> (2012, p. 12)

Following is a list of some of the instructional principles that have come from these three sources. These ideas are fully described and discussed in the 2012 article, but are summarised below.

1. Begin a lesson with a short review of previous learning.
2. Present new material in small steps with student practice after each step.
3. Ask a large number of questions and check the responses of all students.
4. Provide models.
5. Guide student practice.
6. Check for student understanding.
7. Obtain a high success rate.
8. Provide scaffolds for difficult tasks.
9. Require and monitor independent practice.
10. Engage students in weekly and monthly review.

(Rosenshine, 2012)

These ten principles are a feature of how aspects of history are delivered based on the core considerations Rosenshine outlines. For instance, a popular phrase is: 'You don't know what you don't know!' Put simply, if this is the first time a child encounters a concept, a period of history or an individual, asking what they would like to know is unlikely to lead to clear and historically valid questions that lead what comes next.

Beyond this initial teaching phase, supporting children to both transfer what has been learned into the long-term memory and access it is a core feature of how and why lessons are structured the way they are. Retrieval practice is now a common feature in many classrooms and the book series by history teacher Kate Jones (2021, 2022) has been incredibly helpful in embedding several of Rosenshine's principles. This is further explored in Chapter 13.

HOW DOES THIS IMPACT THE NATURE OF HOW I PLAN AND TEACH HISTORY?

Within this particular book, I will be referencing several pieces of this research deliberately and specifically including why I approach activities or lessons in that way. To me, that is how research works best. It interacts with my classroom experience, personal beliefs and individual context of the school I teach in to support my ability to best teach the pupils in my class and support them in gaining an ever-increasing understanding of the curriculum and therefore the wider world. A short summary is found in Table 6.1.

Table 6.1 Summary of research

Research	Influence	Where it is found
Willingham	Ensuring that meaning is clear for children to make it more likely they remember what has been taught Using enquiry questions as a form of problem to create intrigue and the pleasurable rush of solving it at the end	Chronology Enquiry questions
Sweller	Focusing on presenting information clearly and simply Being conscious not to cause cognitive overload in explanations, visual models and tasks	Every facet in terms of how that information is introduced
Rosenshine	Teaching in small steps Selecting a model of delivery based on what the children know Scaffold support for children to facilitate success	Narrating timelines How history lessons are begun Delivering new content in an instructive model
Retrieval practice	Ensure relevant prior knowledge is activated in order to strengthen the child's mental schemata	During history lessons to connect existing knowledge to new learning

SUBJECT-SPECIFIC RESEARCH

There is a wealth of subject-specific history research conducted by practising teachers, subject associations and academics. These offer an insight into how history as a school subject and discipline in its own right has developed over time in order to better support children's growing understanding. One of the best parts of the history teacher community is how rich and supportive it is. On a personal level, I am eternally grateful to those voices I have heard from being a student, a student teacher, a history lead and now in my current role. As a teacher, I am constantly having my eyes opened to the richness of the past and how teachers can teach a range of powerful narratives. Throughout the book you will see references to people like Ian Dawson, Christine Counsell, Beverley Forrest, Sue Temple, Richard Kennett and Andrew Wrenn. This is just a small selection of those that could have been included; they all play a contributing role in my history teaching. When their names are mentioned, it is in a specific context but their work is always worth seeking out where you can.

SUMMARY

When starting out as a primary teacher or history subject lead, it can be overwhelming thinking about what to do, in what order and where to get information from. As summarised from Rosenshine (2012), above:

1. Begin a lesson with a short review of previous learning.

2. Present new material in small steps with student practice after each step.

Specifically, this helps us to ground where we are and start to consider what next. Don't try and do everything at once, especially with a teacher's timetable and workload. If this book prompts further reading, brilliant (it's what I hope happens), but pick your moments and pieces, and don't throw out the baby with the bathwater. Your experience matters and is valuable alongside making use of the available research and evidence.

7

HOW I STRUCTURE UNITS OF HISTORY

BEFORE WE START ...

- Currently, does your school have a model for sequencing lessons in history (or the wider foundation curriculum)?
- If so, how is it implemented across school and why?
- To what extent do you embed links from other subjects into history units of work?
- What value do you feel they add?

MY SEQUENCE OF LESSONS

Figure 7.1 offers an approximate guide for the sequence of lessons I would teach in primary history. It's important to understand that there are always variations based on the number of enquiry questions (see Chapter 11) and working within whole-school pedagogy. The intention with this guide is that it is a starting point which has a clear vision and narrative arc running through it. Tweaking to your school's approach is absolutely needed. The core elements are expanded in subsequent chapters.

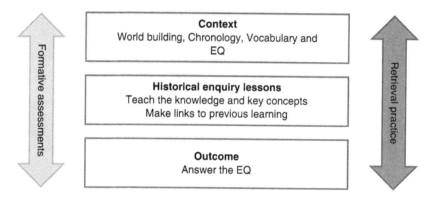

Figure 7.1   A graphic on how this approach looks

THREE PHASES

The unit of history is broken into three broad phases which all vary in length. It is for the individual school and teacher to allot time for each phase to ensure their children have sufficient exposure to the core knowledge to be studied as a focus and the wider sense of period that is crucial to provide meaning to the core. When planning, think of the phases as interlinked and all playing a role in exploring and understanding the narratives we are choosing to emphasise. None of the phases work effectively in isolation so please do not see them as token gestures – they all play an important role.

The terms 'substantive' and 'disciplinary knowledge' feature throughout subsequent chapters and can be easily misunderstood and misapplied. For reference, Counsell (2018b) defined them as follows:

- **Substantive knowledge** is the content that teachers teach as established fact – whether common convention, concept or warranted account of reality.
- **Disciplinary knowledge**, by contrast, is a curricular term for what pupils learn about how that knowledge was established, its degree of certainty and how it continues to be revised by scholars, artists or professional practice.

Substantive knowledge can be broken down into two individual parts. First, individual facts such as the ones I will use in the two worked examples (e.g. the Roman Emperor Claudius ordered the invasion of Britain in 43AD). This is specific to that period; however, the underlying concept of the role of a monarch or an invasion would be encountered across units of history. It is a broad overlapping idea which is a substantive concept.

In subsequent chapters, this will form the basis of how they are used. Substantive knowledge is what is taught in terms of historical 'fact' and broad concepts which span across the full curriculum. Disciplinary knowledge is how that knowledge will be utilised in a history-focused context.

CONTEXT

To children, history is full of abstract settings, characters, lives and events taking place in a world that is alien to their sphere of understanding. It's similar to the amazing realms of fiction they encounter on a daily basis. The early chapters of books introduce this as must we. Something we need to do in history is known as developing a 'sense of period'. It is key because the past was different on so many levels; we need a wider sense of life at the time. This allows children to look at motivations, key decisions and changes with an understanding of the world they took place in, not just from their own 21st-century view of what life is and should be. This phase is multi-disciplinary by its very nature and is where primary pedagogy shines.

By the end of this, the children have a sense of the world they will be learning about in terms of both where and when. Then, domain-specific vocabulary that children will definitely meet is introduced. This is important to front load to provide a reference point to what children are unlikely to have encountered in everyday life. Finally, enquiry questions are introduced which guide the subsequent lessons and the learning which will be core to the final outcome.

HISTORICAL ENQUIRY LESSONS

Bizarrely, this subheading was a difficult one to finalise. The difference between a history lesson and another foundation curriculum lesson can be harder to define in primary than in secondary education. Because a teacher has control over the full curriculum and not just one small piece, effective cross-curricular links are a core feature of primary pedagogy. It's one of the reasons I will argue vehemently that primary schools are not just mini-secondaries. We do things differently: that is, not better or worse, just making the most of the time we have.

Historical enquiry lessons focus on adding a greater depth of both substantive and disciplinary knowledge linked to the enquiry questions which lead the children's learning. Throughout these lessons, the facts and discipline of history are prime considerations. As part of the wider curriculum, other subjects can be linked effectively but the disciplinary aspects will vary. At this stage, the children should encounter a range of voices as any historian would (obviously at an age-appropriate level). Then, begin to consider how that evidence forms our understanding, limitations of that understanding and other pertinent questions. The purpose is not to rewrite history as some may claim but rather present a rich, detailed and representative narrative arc.

Primary teachers are well versed in using historical fiction to supplement children's understanding and weaving the fictional alongside factual historical narratives. Non-fiction writing linked to the leading subject is commonplace too – each of these adds breadth to the children's sense of time, place and period. The wider cross-curricular links may not work in tandem with the history lessons and that is fine. What matters is the value added by each lesson to construct a picture with sufficient clarity for a valid outcome activity.

OUTCOME

To put it simply: if we ask a question, it ought to be answered – otherwise what was the point of the question?

This is the end point for the unit of work by which children have the chance to demonstrate what they've learned in both a substantive and disciplinary sense. The purpose here is to showcase what they know and remember, but it also marks the beginning of the historian's craft.

There is no singular way to answer an enquiry question and it would be wrong for me to claim otherwise. Instead, core principles can be adhered to for children to showcase the learning without it being reduced to something so easily described as style over substance.

RETRIEVAL PRACTICE AND FORMATIVE ASSESSMENT

These are features of all history lessons in one form another. In short, retrieval practice activates prior knowledge which can then be built upon in the lesson. This can take the form of a low-stakes quiz, brain dump or in many other forms. This is valuable in order to strengthen the children's mental schema. While the examples I use tie into the worked units, retrieval practice should be used after the unit of work has been completed to support children in remembering more of what has been learned over time.

Formative assessments take many forms but the key change in my approach over recent years has been away from task completion and accomplishing what I wanted them to and towards whether they have learned the knowledge I intended them to. This knowledge is what plays a critical role in the outcomes at the end of units of history.

WORKED EXAMPLES

The final chapters of the book are two developed examples (one for each key stage) of what this can look like in a primary classroom. They follow the approach advocated for in this book with supporting explanation of why those decisions were made in a wider context. To enable links to be made to previous learning, I have created a fictional curriculum based on a common primary curriculum model. It is ONE option and not THE option for curriculum sequencing.

In no way, shape or form should these examples be viewed as pickup and play units of work because the role of locality and context of an individual school are always key considerations. I have used examples from my own teaching for this purpose – see Chapter 5 for further information on what this could look like.

A POSSIBLE CURRICULUM

To enable me to include conceptual links, there is a loosely defined long-term plan (Table 7.1). The purpose is to highlight how knowledge can be activated, built upon and connected more readily within the worked examples. Once again, this is a long-term plan based on popular selections from the curriculum and is not the definitive sequencing – especially if your school has mixed-age classes. There is no reason to amend yours if it differs.

You can also see that there are two studies in Key Stage 1 and 2 which are defined as 'short studies'. This is when they have been deliberately placed separately from a subsequent unit and could work in tandem with a complementary geography unit. There is no reason a unit of history must cover an entire half-term. Put simply, if it can be taught in sufficient depth and quality in three or four weeks, why wouldn't you? The curriculum is crowded enough without enforcing arbitrary extensions on units of history.

NB Local history is included as individual units and also linked where relevant. The individual units are not expressed in more detail because they are dependent on your school's locality. The non-European and post-1066 studies are not specified because there are many choices that would work alongside the other units in question.

Table 7.1 Long-term plan example

	Autumn	Spring	Summer
EYFS	• Festivals through the year e.g. Christmas, Diwali, Eid, Easter etc. • Stories with historical settings such as fairy tales • Dates commemorated through the year e.g. bonfire night, remembrance and harvest festivals • Observable change in the children's locality • How they have changed from birth to now		
Year 1	Changes within living memory – toys	Significant individual – explorers	Local history
Year 2	Short studies – Moina Michael linked to remembrance – gunpowder plot	Event beyond living memory – first flight	Queen Victoria
Year 3	Local history	Stone Age	Bronze and Iron Age
Year 4	Short study – Roman Empire Roman Britain	Short study – earliest civilisations overview	Ancient Egypt
Year 5	Anglo-Saxon settlement	Anglo-Saxon and Viking conflict	Non-European study
Year 6	Local history – linked to remembrance	Ancient Greek civilisation Ancient Greek influence	Post-1066 study

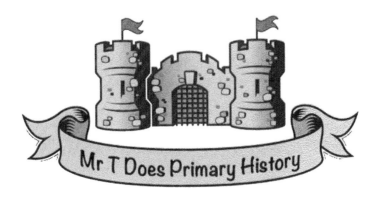

8

CONTEXT: WORLD-BUILDING

BEFORE WE START ...

Think about the Romans and make a list of the first five things that come into your head.

I'll venture a guess that gladiators and the colosseum will feature on the majority of lists, alongside the big hitters like the mighty legions marching across Britain in the 1st century AD. These are snapshots and are a great starting point but have huge limitations in the sense of period children form. Now, think about the world in which those people and events took place? How confident do you feel in placing those choices in the world in which they happened?

A MISTAKE I MADE IN THE PAST

Every topic would start with a launch point ... that quintessential primary school hook day (*aka* wow day, stunning start etc.). We spent huge amounts of time working on a special day to kick the topic off with a bang and hook the children in for the rest of the topic. As an idea, I have no problem with this approach, but the mistake comes from something that didn't happen. If this day doesn't play a core role through the rest of the unit of work, is it as valuable as it could be? I would argue no.

The context phase of the teaching sequence can produce an effective hook because the emphasis is on immersing children in the abstract historical world they will learn about. However, this world remains the core focus for the remainder of the unit of work and therefore the value is not lost. There are many approaches to the concept of a hook day and I will suggest an approach in the KS2 worked example that I feel both inspires curiosity and investment but also maintains a balance between fun and historical understanding.

WHAT DO WE MEAN BY 'WORLD-BUILDING'?

A useful analogy to begin with is the purpose of the early chapters of a fictional story. It introduces the reader to a world that is different to their own, a world that fundamentally impacts the narrative that follows. History is no different! Right at the start, a huge thank you must go to secondary history teacher, Mike Hill, whose blog fundamentally shifted my thinking on the role of world-building. It can be found on Twitter at the top of his page: @michaeldoron

It is a concept I have unintentionally been teaching since my teaching career started. The value of it, however, was not something I was conscious of until much more recently when I considered how children can develop a wider sense of period beyond the core knowledge taught in history lessons. The teacher supports the children in building the abstract world that their learning will take place in. I advocate for this to a be delivered as a direct instruction-style lesson where we immerse children within that world. When done well, this supports children to place their history lessons within the time and place it occurred.

Mike Hill wrote:

> History, after all, is rooted in time and place: if pupils are to understand past events and processes, they must first be able to make sense of the places in which they unfold.
>
> (2020)

In primary history, this is no different and potentially more powerful given that the children's knowledge base is at an earlier stage of development. There are many rich opportunities to make valuable cross-curricular links here to incorporate the first and sixth of Rosenshine's principles (see Chapter 6). Two key advantages of front loading this hinterland knowledge are that it sparks children's curiosity in a way that can be tapped into later and enables the teacher to identify misconceptions about that period as part of the process. For instance, a misconception I have encountered while teaching is that children have believed that post-invasion everyone who was a Briton 'transformed' into a Roman; this is not true and can be explored and clarified in the context of the building process.

Core links to establish:

- physical geography, including any key features that children must understand – e.g. the features of a river when teaching about ancient civilisations
- societal structure and organisation
- cultural beliefs and the role they played in how people lived
- any historical factors (civilisations, groups, individuals, events etc.) (this will be part of the timeline lesson but establishing here is useful if the link is pertinent).

There are a number of resources which can be used to support this – for example, videos from sources such as BBC Teach and Bitesize. Not only do these present simple narratives that can be used to highlight important aspects of setting, also they can often be freely accessible to children outside school. When using sources like this, I usually play them twice, with a different emphasis each time:

1) allow children to just watch to enjoy and immerse;

2) add in simple questions of what to look out for in order to emphasise key aspects that will be relevant in subsequent teaching or are key to life during that period.

THE ROLE GEOGRAPHY PLAYS

Physical geography and human development are interwoven. The nature of the natural world has implications for how humanity develops in different locations across the world. It's why many cross-curricular links add value between the two branches of the humanities.

> Take a minute and think about the geographic features that play a role in the development of the Roman Empire. Then, imagine not teaching them explicitly in the context of the empire's expansion. What misconceptions may arise? I imagine it would be quite a few. Without a more secure grounded understanding of Europe, the expansion of the empire across it is harder to comprehend and that's before we start to consider the geographic features such as the Rhine, Alps and Mediterranean ... within the worked example in this book, I've attempted to include the ones I consider most pertinent.

In the Key Stage 1 worked example, the emphasis is different because the children need to be exposed to the fact that much of what they take as normal didn't exist just over a century ago: no digital technology, cars were incredibly new and rare to see, communication was done via letter or telegram normally. Without exposure to these core concepts, the accomplishment is lessened. The fact it was the first powered flight is an important place to start ... before this, no one had managed it successfully. To an adult, that may seem an obvious point. But, to a young child, this needs explicitly introducing. Once the children learn the Wright brothers flew at Kitty Hawk, introducing the physical geography of the area can help them orientate this setting within the historical story they are learning.

UTILISING THE WORLD

If we consistently retrieve our knowledge of the world the children learn about, new knowledge is more efficiently contextualised. For instance, think about Boudicca's revolt. An over-simplified view is that the Britons were a homogeneous group and all reacted by fighting against the Romans as they conquered their way across England and Wales. Before the relevant lesson on the revolt, the teacher can retrieve the knowledge around Britain being home to numerous Iron Age tribes. Therefore, children are less likely to see this as a singular narrative. As the children learn more about the expansion of the Romans and the Romanisation of Britain, they can grasp this as a time when many different facets of life changed for the people, as well as many aspects of the landscape.

A mainstay of many primary schools is linking a fictional text to their topic. This provides additional richness to the narratives being told as it adds another important story element to history. As Willingham (2021) wrote, stories are psychologically privileged and teachers should use this to help children develop that all-important sense of time and place but, more than this, help them to remember more about the historical realms they are encountering. When there is a natural overlap between what is read in the story and the history lessons that run alongside, prompt the connection and the fact the author must have researched it to present a narrative as correct as possible. Once again, this offers another opportunity to add richness and valuable hinterland knowledge in a purposeful and engaging way.

WHY DOES THIS MATTER?

Dawson (2009, p. 50) points out:

> as experienced historians, we tend to take for granted both our structural map of the past and our rich descriptions of different periods. The ability to draw generalisations about certain periods is arguably just as vital as recognising the diversity within that period.

The implication of this is that identifying that sense of period is of high importance alongside what could be labelled as 'unique' for each period. The Ofsted 2021 research review (2021b) also states:

> Chronological knowledge is also highly generative. Understanding the broad characteristics of historical periods gives context to what pupils learn and can increase pupils' familiarity with new material. Securing overview knowledge of the past supports pupils to develop this knowledge into coherent narratives that are more memorable for them.

This is why both world-building and chronology are core features of the context phase of this particular teaching model. They weave together to help lay foundational understanding to build upon.

From a primary perspective, actively teaching children about the abstract world and using it throughout the sequence in the same way as a fictional setting supports this. Enhancing it with carefully selected historical fiction allows the sense of period to be developed throughout. No story would function fully without a developed setting ... history is a narrative subject after all.

SUMMARY

When thinking about your next unit of history, what do children need to know about the world in which it takes place?
   Key points to consider:

- where in the world is it geographically?
- what is that region of the world like in a physical geographic sense?
- are there any key features which play a key role in what is to be taught?
- how was society organised ... if it was at all?
- given the narratives we are studying, what is key to establish from the outset?

9

CONTEXT: VOCABULARY

BEFORE WE START ...

Imagine you're teaching the Romans next; make a list of the vocabulary your children will need to understand in order for the history lessons to proceed.

- Consider why you chose those words?
- What merit is there in knowing them in advance?

WHERE HAVE I GONE WRONG?

I have always attempted to teach children the vocabulary they were encountering in their history lessons. My mistakes lay in the way in which I enacted this:

1. spelling tests of relevant linked words without considering meaning sufficiently
2. selecting words from a printable list without fully considering the role they played in my history lessons
3. asking the children to create their own word lists using dictionary definitions.

VOCABULARY VS SUBSTANTIVE CONCEPTS

Something that can get so very easily confused is the difference between vocabulary and a substantive concept. It is an easy thing to get mixed up. Later in this chapter, there is an example of a substantive concept progression for the concept of monarchy as a system of government. Within that concept, the children will get repeated exposures to the different ways we may express this such as a king, queen, pharaoh etc. The exposure to the vocabulary will not just arise through history lessons either because the role of monarchs is commonplace in stories they will be read or read themselves.

As the children encounter the vocabulary repeatedly, we can introduce the substantive concept of monarchy and begin to examine the nuanced features of this system of government.

DIFFERENT TYPES OF VOCABULARY

The vocabulary we teach can be classified in different ways, including verbs, nouns, adjectives etc. that children will be taught from a very young age. When thinking about the teaching of primary history, Beck, McKeown and Kucan's Tiers of Language model (2002) is a useful start point.

They identified three tiers of language:

Tier 1: These are words used in everyday speech and appear in conversations. They are frequently encountered so are unlikely to require specific instruction. In primary history, these can be the base level of words children may use to describe an artefact or a person when they first encounter them.

Tier 2: These could be described as mature and more formal words that are useful across subjects. These words are useful to support the clarity of explanation and especially evidence-based reasoning using language such as to contradict or offer alternate perspectives to consider varied viewpoints.

Tier 3: These are domain- or subject-specific words that do not occur often and are best introduced in specific contexts as they occur. Words such as pharaoh, hierarchy and polytheism would come within this tier.

WHEN AND HOW WILL WE INTRODUCE IT

Tier 2 and 3 vocabulary are going to form the backbone of the language that is introduced. However, because of their differing function, the manner and time they are going to be introduced will differ. Within the two worked examples, the tier 3 words are identified and play a core role in the substantive knowledge to be taught. They are also specifically stated as a part of the National Curriculum in aim 3. Substantive concepts can act as a way in which individual tier 3 words or phrases can be linked across units of history. Tier 2 will be used more actively in individual lessons in order to model how that term can be used in oral or written answers. They provide a toolkit that children can draw upon when attempting to either explain their personal viewpoints or answer as a historian might.

TO KNOWLEDGE ORGANISER OR NOT TO KNOWLEDGE ORGANISER

In recent years, the knowledge organiser has become a common feature of many primary classrooms up and down the country. This growth in popularity runs in parallel to the greater consideration given to cognitive science. If schools choose to make use of knowledge organisers, they are where tier 3 words can be first introduced in the context phase of the teaching sequence. Their potential value was summarised by Jon Hutchinson (no date) as:

1. a planning tool, setting out all of the core, foundational facts that must be learned to understand and master a particular topic
2. an assessment tool, allowing you throughout a unit of work to quickly check that pupils are learning exactly what you hoped they would
3. perhaps most powerfully, is the knowledge organiser's function as a quizzing tool, helping pupils to recall with lightning speed the key information needed to make sense of the topic.

However, to make the most of knowledge organisers, it's key that children are taught how to use them and why they are useful in lessons. Is it fair to say they can add value to the curriculum? Absolutely. For the purpose of this particular chapter, they are a brilliant reference point for core facts and definitions that matter based on what the children will learn. Secondary teacher Ashley Bartlett described their function eloquently in a virtual teachmeet in 2021. He said they provide the minimum children must master so that future teaching can build, develop and strengthen understanding (TeachMeet, 2021).

In a vocabulary sense, what knowledge organisers allow teachers to do is provide clarity over the language children will encounter with a security blanket that they know what it means. One potential difficulty is that children who struggle with reading or are still focusing on decoding will find this immensely challenging and therefore need structured scaffolds and support as Rosenshine (2012) suggests. Think carefully about which year groups will use knowledge organisers as they are not a one-size-fits-all model.

Are lists the most effective ways of presenting all types of information? No. Reif (cited in Caviglioli and Goodwin, 2021) highlighted the relative merits of lists networks and hierarchies. Lists are:

Familiar and useful for remembering steps of a sequence but not for identifying links between concepts and ideas.

This is important to remember: that they are a tool of value but must be built on. Subsequent teaching must reinforce these links to ensure they are made. It's one of the reasons why I use a range of graphic organisers in lessons to arrange the information appropriately.

In summary, knowledge organisers are a useful tool when used appropriately (aren't most things?) but don't use them entirely because someone said you should. Use them with purpose, clarity and a clear sense of the value that they add. However, be wary of teaching the vocabulary on them in isolation as context is key. Don't just use them once and then expect children to access and navigate across them ... repeated exposures!

SUBSTANTIVE CONCEPT SPECIFICITY

Something to be wary of was identified by Ofsted in their 2021 research review:

> Substantive concepts are not simply 'definitions' of important terms. They have particular meanings in different contexts. First, they have a particular meaning when used in the context of a historical narrative or argument. Second, they often have meanings that are specific to particular periods or places.
>
> (2021d)

The implication of this is that even though it may be efficient to have a generic definition for a concept which is placed on the knowledge organiser that is consistent across school, it can be problematic because the important levels of specificity can be lost. A better approach would be to provide a specific definition in the relevant context and then support children to connect it to the wider substantive concept it links to.

Think of a definition of the word 'monarch'. The dictionary defines it as a person who rules a country – for example, a king or a queen. This is a reasonable start point for younger children when first introduced to the concept via a story in EYFS or learning about a significant individual in Key Stage 1. It's an entry point but as children progress through school, the meaning changes depending upon which period they are studying, as explored in Table 9.1.

The variation between what children will understand or learn at different stages of their education is how the individual vocabulary and associated meanings connect together to form an understanding of the broader substantive concept.

Table 9.1 Specific aspects of monarch that are pertinent during different units studied

EYFS	KS1	LKS2	UKS2
... character is a king This means they are the most important in the kingdom They live in a castle	The king had absolute power in Britain in 1605 He didn't let Catholics worship as they wanted to Head of the Church of England	Iron Age Britain Ruled over an area of land Many across Britain of differing sizes and levels of power	Early Medieval Britain Led by monarchs Monarchs held varied amounts of land in their kingdoms Anglo-Saxon kings elected by a council called the Witan
I am a queen (said in role walking round in costume)	Queen Victoria ruled over the United Kingdom and the British Empire	The Roman Empire The emperor was a form of monarch They held absolute power	Non-European study*
Guy Fawkes wanted to blow up the king		Roman Britain Contrasting role of Boudicca/ Cartimandua and the emperor	Ancient Greek city-states Each city-state had a different government Some had monarchs Sparta had dual kings Athens was home to the world's first democracy
		Ancient Egypt Held absolute power Governed in dynasties Head of state and also high priest of all the temples	Post-1066**

Notes: *content depends on if the Maya, Benin or Early Islamic history is chosen. All were led by a form of monarchy but the nuance is hugely varied.
** the role of a monarch would be limited to certain studies and potentially not mentioned in others.

While this is not an exhaustive list and, to a large extent, depends on the core knowledge as defined by the enquiry question, it hopefully highlights that a king is more than just the person in charge. However we present the vocabulary, it's important to emphasise that the definition works within the historical context.

DISCIPLINARY LANGUAGE

Disciplinary concepts are often referred to as second-order concepts because they guide how we make use of the substantive knowledge (first-order). In a vocabulary sense, children will once again learn these through repeated encounters. They play a key role in the way in which enquiry questions are crafted, which is further explored in Chapter 11. Hodkinson (2012) wrote about the different types of chronological vocabulary children may need to use and its importance in having a much greater appreciation of the past:

1. descriptive vocabulary such as before, after and ancient
2. technical vocabulary such as AD, BC and nineteenth century for the year 1845
3. conceptual vocabulary such as change, continuity, period, chronology.

It is important to remember that these terms have a different function in history but children will need to hear these terms used in context, have their own use scaffolded and opportunities to practise saying or writing in context.

WHY DOES IT MATTER?

The children are going to encounter vocabulary in every lesson and it plays a core role in what the children will learn and how they will express that understanding. Quigley (2018) wrote about the importance of children being encouraged to read, speak and write like historians. It enables children to express their thinking in a clearer and more precise manner. Fidler (2020, p. 33) wrote:

> Identifying a clear progression for children's learning and use of historical vocabulary supports them in continually building

their historical knowledge and understanding and has an invaluable contribution to make to all areas of the history curriculum.

The reason it matters is that it has an impact on children's ability to understand individual units of history and also the way in which they can connect broader substantive concepts which span across the history curriculum which is specified in Key Stage 2's subject content paragraph.

SUMMARY

Vocabulary and substantive concepts are different things. It's important they are not conflated. Think carefully about which specific vocabulary is embedded in each unit of history and why it 'matters'.

- In which lessons etc. will the children encounter those words?
- How can they build on what is previously known?
- Which substantive concepts do they align with?
- Are the children given the opportunity to use the language in a range of scaffolded contexts?

Mr T Does Primary History

10

CONTEXT: CHRONOLOGY

BEFORE WE START ...

Think about what the teaching of chronology looks like in your classroom. Specifically, the following:

- What do you want the children to know by the end of it?
- What will the children do during the lesson and how is it set up?
- What prerequisite knowledge and understanding from other subjects do they need to have in order for the lesson to work?
- What role does it play within subsequent lessons?

These are the foundational questions that have come to shape the way in which I teach and think about chronology in primary history. Through this chapter, I'll elaborate on the importance of considering these factors and more.

WHERE HAVE I GONE WRONG?

In the past, many chronology mistakes have been made. I don't have time to explain all of them now so I'm just giving some overall themes that didn't serve me as well as I thought they did. The example later in the chapter is also something I've done on several occasions.

1. Sequencing is part of chronology but is not the ultimate stage of development.
2. Chronology is too complex to just do once.
3. What am I going to do with my timeline once it's made?

WHAT IS CHRONOLOGY?

Start by thinking about the Greek etymology of history again where the word narrative appears. History is a narrative subject driven by rich and varied stories. This means chronology is going to have a central role in telling and unpicking those stories.

The dictionary defines 'chronology' as the arrangement of events or dates in the order of their occurrence. It sounds so simple, doesn't it? While the overall idea is relatively simple, anyone who has attempted to teach it will know that absolutely isn't the case. Chronology is complex and underpinned by various mathematical concepts around place value, measurement, numerical scales and how we depict different aspects of the past that have wildly differing durations. Can you imagine teaching number bonds or times tables by reciting them once? That sounds ludicrous! However, if we teach one arbitrary chronology lesson at the start of each unit of history in isolation, that's what can so easily happen.

Phillips (2008, p. 42) defined chronology as having a dual purpose in history teaching, writing that:

Chronology is a key organising tool for developing pupils' understanding of history and as a 'concept' within the history curriculum.

It's important that teachers use this to inform not only what the timelines look like but how the lesson itself is taught. This dual purpose, alongside the need to reduce the possibility of cognitive overload, is why I use two separate timelines to create a fuller picture of history. This is explained in more detail later in the chapter.

HOW HAS THIS LOOKED FOR ME IN THE PAST?

A common chronology lesson … the teacher has printed and cut out picture cards from a resource website. The children are sat in groups of between four and six. The instruction is given to the class to sequence the cards chronologically and they dutifully attempt to do this.

The teacher works the room, meticulously documenting the task that is being completed with photographs of busy children. Let's say Group 1 have made a mistake around an event that's BC and another that's AD. Because the teacher has five groups to get around, they correct it without unpacking the misconception fully. Group 2 finish quickly and Group 3 are arguing about the joy that is playground football. Group 4 have a simplified version to complete as this lesson is differentiated by task.

As each group finishes, they have the classic photograph showing two thumbs up at a task well done.

Take a minute to read through that scenario again. What misconceptions may have arisen? What difficulties could the teacher encounter? Most importantly, what happens next?

HOW SHOULD IT BE TAUGHT?

Let's start by breaking chronology into smaller composite parts. This supports Rosenshine's 2012 Principles of Instruction and enables the teacher to see chronology as a series of steps leading to an outcome. In addition, as the children become more fluent with each step, the teacher can progress through them or begin to apply them to different contexts. To this end, I break the process of constructing a timeline down into a series of concepts to build towards aim 1 of the NC: 'know and understand the history of these islands as a coherent, chronological narrative'. This can be seen in Table 10.1.

Table 10.1   Chronology broken into composite steps

Sequencing	Placing events/people etc. in a chronological order
Scale	Using a mathematical scale on the timeline. The scale varies depending on content but is pre-requisite for subsequent steps
Interval	The 'gap' between events, periods etc.
Duration	The amount of time a period, event, lifetime took place for
Concurrent	Two people, periods, events happening at the same point in history. The duration does not need to be identical for them to be concurrent
Interacted	This builds on the understanding of concurrence. The concept that groups can exist at the same point in history is different to saying that they encountered each other. Once it has been established that they did encounter each other, in what ways did the encounters happen?

These steps allow a teacher to introduce concepts at an age-appropriate level, then emphasise those that are most critical to unpick the particular narratives being taught. For instance, when Year 3 encounter the Stone Age to Iron Age unit the key concept is the immense duration of the palaeolithic period – around 2.5 million years.

Now that the core concept has been established, which approach to teaching should be utilised? Given that this is a complex and key concept for history, I will always push towards a model of direct instruction unless children are immensely familiar with constructing timelines. As Willingham (2009, p. 87) writes, 'Discovery learning has much to recommend it, when it comes to the level of student engagement.' This initially sounds positive and a useful way to hook children in but he adds, 'An important downside, however, is that what students will think about is less predictable' (2009, p. 87). When the teacher instructs students, they can focus attention on what is truly important and it is more likely it will be learned. In core lessons, often teach using the model of I do, we do then you do ... why not apply this across the curriculum? It is beneficial in many cases beyond this isolated example.

No longer will the task be differentiated for the children as my intention is for them all to reach the same result – a timeline which clearly depicts the narratives that make up the core knowledge. There may be some occasions where this isn't appropriate for a small number of children who have specific SEND but this would be the exception to the rule and not the norm. This is exemplified in the two worked examples.

MATHEMATICAL UNDERPINNING

The prehistory in Year 3 example (Table 10.2) has been deliberately selected because it illustrates one aspect of chronology which can truly cause problems in the classroom. The mathematical underpinning needed to make sense of timelines as a graphic organiser. Something I wish I had realised earlier in my career was how laden with maths chronology is beyond simple numerical values. In Table 10.2, there are some important ideas which I now feel are important to acknowledge and, where possible, mitigate. One thing that truly stands out is the important role of considering which knowledge is perquisite to lessons beyond the isolated domain of history.

Table 10.2 Common mathematical problems and links I have encountered

Potential misconception	Mathematical concept	Mitigations
The Great Fire of London happened in 1666. What does this mean? The Palaeolithic is 2.5 million years. What does this mean?	Place value	Use a physically accurate scale to give the 'gist' of what is being depicted. E.g. how much jumps from now to the first flight? 4 jumps. How much jumps from now to the Great Fire of London? 15 jumps. The association is further away in distance from now shows that it is further into the past. Support the children in understanding using a suitable reference such as constructing it physically on the playground and using it as context alongside explanation. On this metre stick, the palaeolithic is 99cm 9mm. While not a precise explanation, the scale clearly depicts the palaeolithic is much greater than everything else in human history.

(Continued)

Table 10.2   Continued

Potential misconception	Mathematical concept	Mitigations
Confusing BC/BCE and AD/CE or finding the scale itself confusing	Negative number	Before learning negative number. Emphasise the fact that 'B' means before so the children can orientate it means before Christians believe Jesus was born. Once this has been learned, activate the mathematical link to what they know and model carefully.
Struggling to construct the timeline along the scale efficiently within a lesson	Lack of mathematical fluency over place value or calculations	Do they need to construct the timeline independently? Not at all, it can be heavily scaffolded where they complete a model that has been started. Alternatively, provide them with the model and spend the lesson on unpicking what it represents. Can the scale use concrete resources to scaffold children's understanding? Yes, multilink in Key Stage 1 and metre sticks for Key Stage 2 are something I find very useful.

TWO TYPES OF TIMELINE

In a quest to avoid cognitive overload, I introduce children to two different types of timeline:

- overall narrative or big picture of 'everything'
- internal narrative of what is to be taught subsequently.

The two types serve different purposes and allow me to emphasise different things. They also enable me to mitigate the fact that 'working memory is the bottleneck of our thinking' as Oliver Lovell (2020, p. 19) wrote in relation to cognitive load. By separating this out, the working memory doesn't have to focus on so many pieces of the puzzle at once.

The big picture timeline for Key Stage 2 (Figure 10.1) presents the complete narrative of the taught curriculum children will see. This is an aspect of chronology specified in both Key Stage 1 and 2 in the NC14.

It provides a general overview from which prior learning can be retrieved and connections made to subsequent learning. By introducing this first, children can be supported in placing their new learning into a clearer context of the wider world. In isolation, this introduces children to when in the past this period of history sits, but alongside a world map we can show where. As a pairing, this is incredibly valuable because it serves as a way to emphasise the interactions of human and physical geography including how the latter influences the former, as explored in Chapter 8, World-building. Once this big picture is set, children can zoom in on the internal narrative of a smaller timespan. Ofsted's last subject report, *History for All* (2011), stated,

> They knew about particular events, characters and periods but did not have an overview. Their chronological understanding was often underdeveloped and so they found it difficult to link developments together.

This underpins why the big picture timeline is so key in my teaching.

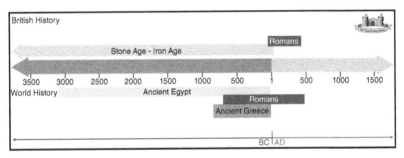

Figure 10.1 Overall narrative timeline for KS2

The internal narrative is important because it sets out the key events, individuals and changes the children are going to be studying. This immediately sets out the core difference between the overall and internal narratives. This is the timeline children tend to construct as it forms the backbone of the teaching sequence. Figure 10.2 shows what it could look like at each stage of the teaching process. Inevitably, how this looks will depend on each school's curriculum sequence and school structure.

Part 1: construction

1. Activate prior knowledge and describe the task
2. Sequence
3. Add a mathematical scale
4. Distribute events accurately along the scale.

Part 2: narration

1. Checking understanding
2. Create meaning, curiosity and intrigue
3. Link and reference the EQ.

Sequencing

Julius Caesar invades Britain. 55 and 54 BC	Claudius orders the invasion of Britain. 43 AD	Roman coloniais founded at Colchester. 49 AD	Boudicca's revolt. 60 to 61 AD	Roman York is founded. c. 71 AD	Hadrian's Wall is built. 122 AD	Britain is raided by Picts, Scots and Anglo-Saxons. c. 360 AD	The Britons are told to look to their own defences. 410 AD

This sequence presents children with a small number of core chronological concepts including how BC/AD or BCE/CE work mathematically. However it is deficient in that it can introduce them to history as a singular narrative of linked events. In this case, some of these events form part of the process of establishing and preserving the Roman presence but this isn't always the case.

Adding a scale

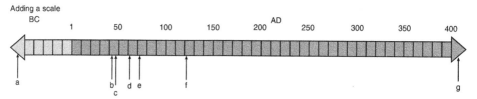

By placing these events onto the timeline, children can identify the varied intervals between them. It opens out the narrative and reduces the likelihood of them presuming a direct link between events when it doesn't exist or establishing the link when it does. However, this timeline must be narrated so children understand the purpose of the arrowheads at either end and, using Dawson's story analogy to explain that children aren't seeing every aspect of Roman Britain on this timeline.

Narrating

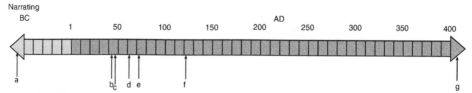

Consider the language children would encounter in this timeline. There will be words they haven't encountered and others which have specific meanings and implications in this particular period. By narrating this, we can model the precise meaning to reduce misconceptions. Also, when events are linked, will children identify and understand this? The cluster of events (b to d) are linked because of the role of Colchester (Camulodunum) in the early conquest.

Figure 10.2   The timeline at each stage of the teaching process

TIME CONSTRAINTS AND PRACTICALITIES

To construct and narrate the timeline is not a quick task and I am conscious of how much foundation curriculum time there is (a topic for another day). If you find yourself short of time, concentrate on the narration phase. This is where meaning and investment is generated and, as Willingham states, something having meaning makes it more likely to be remembered. My personal preference is to narrate it as a story where I can stop on words I know are key and define them in context. These would be those tier 3 words mentioned in Chapter 9. Children can also circle or highlight those they are unsure of for me to define. Doing this as a dictionary task takes longer and is more likely to lead to erroneous definitions.

WHAT NEXT?

If this is constructed and ticked off in one lesson for the benefit of the school's foundation subject tracking spreadsheet, what does it offer? Task completion. When children learn a story, do they look at the narrative arc once? No. Therefore, this shouldn't be the case with the historical narrative the timeline depicts. This is for several important reasons.

1. Context

    Each time something is taught, it can be placed within the wider narrative and linked to what else is known. For the overall narrative timeline, this is a core function as it establishes concurrence. This reduces the chance of children seeing history as a series of unrelated events. It can also help rationalise why that event took place where it did. For instance, a rebellion taking place shortly after an invasion shows the Romans had not secured control of Britain at that stage (see KS2 worked example).

2. Links within and across

    Building on laying the context of when something occurred, links can be made within and across the periods studied as specified in the KS2 National Curriculum. Children can be taught to look for patterns in what they see in front of them to emphasise aspects of the narrative. This may be a conceptual link such as the repeated invasions of Britain from the Romans through to 1066. This can also be featured when looking at the narrative in reverse; as children look further back in time, the teacher can guide them through what they wouldn't see.

3. Change over time and turning points

A core disciplinary concept is continuity and change. This concept can be emphasised by using a timeline as a graphic organiser. Here children can be introduced to when changes took place and then annotate further to look what the changes were and the impact of those changes (see KS1 worked example). Another use can be when a decisive change takes place that is a turning point from which further periods of change take place.

4. Provides a reference point for retrieval practice

When used in conjunction with focused enquiry questions, children can use internal narrative timelines to identify the core knowledge they have gained so far that will be useful in their final answers. Or, when recapping on what was learned previously, teachers can pose retrieval questions such as which other civilisation that we have studied had an empire? Which other periods had a monarchy as their government?

Display the timeline somewhere prominent and make use of it consistently throughout the topic. This allows the children to identify the relative position of each event that they learn.

Some schools choose to buy a bespoke timeline for their hall, playground, classrooms or corridors – potentially your school has one too. The key is how and when are they going to be used. When this isn't considered, you can end up with a beautiful piece of wallpaper or even a stunning work of art – but its primary role can so easily be lost.

SUMMARY

Hopefully, the complexity and central role of chronology is clearer. Remember, don't treat it as one almighty undertaking but rather a number of small steps which lead to a greater sense of understanding.

- What will your timelines look like and why?
- Which concept do you need to begin with?
- Which concept will you emphasise and why?
- How will you build on what the children already know?

The two worked examples in the final two chapters of this book have example timelines for both the overall and internal narrative.

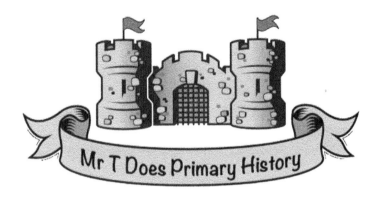

11

WHY HISTORICAL ENQUIRY QUESTIONS ARE HELPFUL

BEFORE WE START ...

There are a number of ways in which a unit of history can be titled or 'led'. If the school follows a topic-led approach, it is more likely to be a more generic title, question or emphasis than what I will be advocating below. Hopefully, what has become clear is that I am not suggesting that history should be taught in isolation in

(Continued)

> primary schools – far from it. Whether topic- or subject-led, using focused enquiry questions to lead the history lessons is a pedagogical approach that will provide a clear emphasis on which knowledge should be taught and also a vehicle for children to continue to develop their disciplinary understanding.

WHERE HAVE I GONE WRONG?

I love a witty pun! Those that know me will wince every time I share my hilarious word play, but they can sometimes feature in topic webs. When I began teaching, topic titles were the mainstay when defining the foundation curriculum. Below are genuine examples that I used in past history topics (and will *not* be using again).

- There's no place like Rome
- Walk Like an Egyptian
- Traders or Invaders?

Be honest, what does it add? The answer is not a huge amount beyond a wry smile, a quick giggle and probably an explanation on the fact 'Walk Like an Egyptian' is a song by the Bangles released in 1986 and the ancient Egyptians didn't walk like that. Puns are great when they are understood on a personal level but humour is so subjective. Another difficulty arises when that's all a teacher is given to guide their foundation curriculum. If that teacher is a non-specialist and has not studied history since Year 9, how can this produce effective and purposeful lesson sequences? Also, are they meeting the curriculum specification? The history curriculum is phrased in such a way as to guide teachers over emphases even though it does not specify precise content.

In other cases, a poorly chosen title can actively reinforce misconceptions or veer lessons towards tangents of little consequence. If I say we are going to be learning about superheroes, I would be astonished if your mind went to Florence Nightingale, Neil Armstrong etc.

In the past, I went wrong by failing to clarify which aspects of the past were going to be central; I used a generic title which led to a scattergun approach to sequencing and failed to balance the roles of substantive and disciplinary knowledge. This is why enquiry questions (EQs) are helpful. Naturally and purposefully, they facilitate both.

WHAT IS HISTORICAL ENQUIRY AND WHY DOES IT MATTER?

In 2018, the Department for Education called for pilot schools to receive curriculum development funds, which specified that they should be structured around teacher-led instruction and not enquiry-based learning. It's important to clarify that historical enquiry is not the same as enquiry-based learning where children discover facts for themselves. The Historical Association clarified the meaning and purpose of enquiry in history which serves as an introductory definition:

> An 'enquiry' in the history education community is shorthand for a sequence of lessons integrated by a direct focus on a single 'enquiry question' and within which pupils build knowledge systematically and cumulatively in order to be able to answer that question by the end of it. A well-crafted enquiry explicitly facilitates a knowledge-rich approach to history and allows the teacher to guide the pupil through complex and contrary histories rather than leaving them to reach ill-informed judgements without adequate knowledge.
>
> (Sullivan, 2018)

A question has a leading role in a series of lessons and we do not teach a separate enquiry per lesson. However, it is absolutely fine to break the overall enquiry question into sub-questions in order to give individual lessons greater clarity.

It's important to consider the role that enquiry plays within the history curriculum. First, historical enquiry is explicitly required in NC aim 5. But, more importantly, using focused, historically valid questions provides a clear emphasis on which aspects of that period, person or event are to be studied in depth. Because the emphasis is clear, teachers can avoid the scattergun approach and ensure children spend sufficient time acquiring, interpreting, discussing etc. the core knowledge for that particular unit of study which children must remember. This was explained in the Ofsted research review for history, which stated:

> High-quality enquiry questions organise historical content to enable pupils to develop disciplinary and substantive knowledge simultaneously, with their understanding of each supporting the other.
>
> (2021d)

In addition to providing clarity, leading the history curriculum with thought-provoking questions works in tandem with Willingham's work on cognitive science in the classroom. He wrote that, from a cognitive perspective, an important factor in how much children like school is whether or not a student consistently experiences the 'pleasurable rush' of solving a problem (2009, p. 1). This is where teachers can add intrigue in a controlled manner while knowing that children will develop sufficient knowledge to have an evidence-led answer by the end of the sequence of lessons.

An important caveat though: core knowledge must not be encountered in isolation. History is a narrative subject, as was explained in the previous chapter, and therefore we must teach that core knowledge within the context that it happened. This is what Christine Counsell (2018) referred to as 'hinterland knowledge'. If history is reduced to a series of isolated facts presented on a knowledge organiser or working wall, the children's understanding will be shallow at best. Counsell identifies that both are equally important. After all, how clear is a narrative if we spend every second on the character's actions, motivations and relationships but no time on the setting and broader world in which it is set? Enquiry questions allow primary teachers to teach the core knowledge in real depth while using the wider curriculum and historical fiction to present the hinterland ... the interconnected primary curriculum in action.

IN THE CLASSROOM

Because the EQ is going to provide a leading role in the teaching sequence, it must be introduced in the context phase. Personally, I introduce it after the children have encountered the historical world they will be learning about and in the same lesson as internal narrative timeline. It needs to maintain a prominent role in subsequent history lessons to support the children in distinguishing between the core and hinterland knowledge. The core knowledge plays a central role in providing the knowledge base in the answer.

When it's introduced, the children need to spend time discussing the meaning of the question and ensuring they have understood what it asks of them. Can the children discern the difference between the trivial and core if they don't have a clear vision on what they are aiming to answer?

Because the enquiry runs over a number of lessons, it also provides an excellent prompt for retrieval. At the start of every lesson, I will ask the children to tell their partner what they have learned already that will be useful in the final answer. This allows me to consider whether the children have retained what I wanted them to and address misconceptions where they arise. It can also be further connected to previous units of history.

At the end of the sequence, the children have acquired the knowledge which is directly related to the enquiry question. The simple outcome is an answer to said question. This is explored in Chapter 14.

WHAT MAKES A GOOD EQ?

Creating purposeful and workable enquiry questions is not an exacting science but more of an art. What stands out for history teaching is that the question must be rooted in the discipline of history and one that a historian could ask. Questions based around a modern perception of the world can, if we are not careful, misrepresent the past or wrongly attribute a set of values on the past that wasn't the case. When I have taught about the Athenian democracy in the past, I have leaned into children's outrage that the democracy was deficient by our 21st-century view of what democracy should be. This instantly created an emotional response in the children that the democracy was not fair and therefore a bad example. What I inadvertently did was use a presentism viewpoint of the concept. Instead of presenting it as a binary choice of fair system and not fair system or now vs then, it's important to view it in different ways.

1. Compared to the Athenian monarchy it replaced, it was more representative and fairer. Therefore, even though it was not fair, children understood it was fairer as more people had a political voice. This can be further compared to other ancient Greek city-states such as the Spartan oligarchy.
2. Introduce the complex concept of democracy as playing a role in the modern world the children encounter, which links to British values. Then, ensure they know that women's enfranchisement is a recent development that occurred just over a century ago. Therefore, what they see as fair today has been shaped over centuries.

The outcome of this is a deeper sense of what the concept of democracy is and how it is not merely a dictionary definition.

Riley (2000) posed three questions that can be used to ascertain whether an enquiry question could be classed as a good one:

Does each of your enquiry questions:

- capture the interest and imagination of your pupils?
- place an aspect of historical thinking, concept or process at the forefront of the pupils' minds?
- result in a tangible, lively, substantial, enjoyable 'outcome activity' (i.e. at the end of the lesson sequence) through which pupils can *genuinely answer* the enquiry question?

(2000, p. 8, emphasis in original)

HOW MANY ENQUIRY QUESTIONS SHOULD WE USE?

A loaded question for sure. It's important that children have sufficient time to learn the substantive knowledge required and also debate, discuss and interpret it to ensure they gain an understanding of sufficient depth. If we think about Riley's third question, to *genuinely answer* the question, the series of lessons must be long enough to provide a clear knowledge base and time to get to grips with the range of sources of evidence studied. Another important factor to consider is how long the school has allocated. If you only have a half-term in which to meet the NC objective, one enquiry may be the maximum possible.

The examples provided in the book break the units of work into several shorter enquiries and provide a greater sense of time and place when viewed as a whole. When using an overall enquiry question, it can seem like a daunting task but this can be broken into sub-questions which can be covered in a lesson.

SUMMARY

Historical enquiry is not only specified in the National Curriculum; it is also a great way in which to provide clarity over what substantive and disciplinary knowledge will be taught during that particular sequence of lessons.

When considering your enquiry question, these prompts are useful reminders:

1. is it meeting Riley's three criteria?

2. is it achievable during the curriculum time available?

3. are there any cross-curricular links which would add value in a supporting role?

4. how can you activate prior knowledge and what are you building towards?

12

TEACHING A *HISTORY* LESSON

BEFORE WE START ...

Out of the list below, which of the following would you define as a history lesson or not a history lesson? Take some time to consider why.

- Making shields
- Making Roman roads out of cake or Stonehenge out of biscuits
- Colouring in
- Reading comprehension
- Making mosaics
- Invading another classroom.

WHERE HAVE I GONE WRONG?

In 2010, when I was bright eyed and full of that NQT vigour, I dived headlong into planning history lessons. I've enjoyed planning it since then as you may have guessed. Some of these lessons I look back at now and wince. Others I still use today in modified forms.

1. A lesson on ancient Egyptian agriculture with an entire emphasis on what the systems in place were. It lacked both why it mattered and how that knowledge had been acquired to our modern eyes.
2. Proudly challenging my Year 6 children to unpick Tacitus' account of Boudicca's speech before the climactic battle of Watling Street. They persevered but I missed out a hugely important step ... more on that later in the chapter.
3. Misunderstanding the role of source material when studying the past.

WHAT IS A HISTORY LESSON?

In *Simplicitus* by Emma Turner (2022, p. 3), Tom Sherrington identifies one important consideration:

> Debates around curriculum design in a primary context are often formulated in terms of a contest between specialist teaching of traditional subject disciplines and a holistic approach made up of broad topics and themes. Of course, a truly great curriculum is a synthesis of these ideas ...

Because of the different curriculum structures primary schools use, this is a challenging question because so many lessons are interwoven around a broader topic heading. As a result, I am drawing a distinction here between building the unit of history work around enquiry questions and those which add that wider sense of breadth and richness to the sense of period. In the worked examples, I have included some cross-curricular links I would make because they add important contextual hinterland knowledge.

Using the ideas laid out in Chapter 2, I am choosing to focus in on lessons that have the following characteristics:

1. Add or interrogate substantive knowledge which will be relevant across the unit using sources of evidence. The knowledge gained across these lessons will form the factual base for the final answer at the end of that part of the sequence.
2. Support the children to have a greater understanding of the discipline of history by using a disciplinary concept to interpret existing or new knowledge.

You may notice these are broad features – which is entirely deliberate. It would be a brave person to give a definite characteristic of what is a history lesson and what isn't. What may be interesting is to look back at the 'Before we start' list with this view in mind. Consider which do and don't fall within these broad parameters ...

WHAT THE CHILDREN WILL LEARN AND DO

Front and centre in many curriculum conversations I have is the distinction between what the children will know and what they will do. In the past, I have veered to what they will do without ample consideration of what they will learn from it ... therefore they had a great time (I hope) but didn't gain a huge amount of purposeful knowledge. The examples at the top of the chapter contain some tasks like this which are popular and fun but heavy on school resources and curriculum time. Can you do them? Absolutely. Should you do them? Context will always be key.

The reading comprehension hopefully prompted some conversations about the role reading plays in the curriculum. Christopher Such (2021) opens his book *The Art and Science of Teaching Primary Reading* with a profound statement 'Few impediments undermine a person's aspirations as effectively as an inability to read' (p. 1). Reading is at the heart of the primary teacher's role and rightly so given how central it is. Many a history lesson will require an element of age-appropriate reading and so use many of the procedural features of a reading comprehension such as the Boudicca example I will explore later in the chapter. What makes a history lesson more than merely a reading comprehension is that the search for 'answers' is rarely a binary choice of right and wrong but shades of grey.

WHY DO SOURCES OF EVIDENCE MATTER?

Sources of evidence are the stuff of history. It's what remains of the past and can create a connection between the 21st century and distant times long forgotten. Genuinely, it's the fun bit of studying the past and the historical discipline. In the Historical Association's 2020 *What's the Wisdom On* ... series, Helen Snelson remarks:

> it's just absolutely magic ... to actually get so excited by touching, engaging, smelling or listening to that remnant of human society gone by and starting to let it speak.
>
> (Burn et al., 2020)

It is also what Helen Carr and Suzannah Lipscomb wrote about as 'the magic, the myth, the stuff we didn't know' (2022, p. 4), to which I referred in Chapter 2. Think about when primary children walk into a castle dungeon, an old mill or realise the document in front of them was produced centuries ago. Those visceral reactions inspire curiosity, prompt questions and connect them to what once was.

Without sources of evidence, there is no history.

THE CONCEPT OF EVIDENCE

Aim 5 of the curriculum specifies the children should:

> understand the methods of historical enquiry, including how evidence is used rigorously to make historical claims, and discern how and why contrasting arguments and interpretations of the past have been constructed.

In each of the examples below, evidence is incorporated as a fundamental part of how the children learn to both study and make sense of the past as part of the enquiries.

To do this, it's important that children are introduced to what a source of evidence can be, the range of them that exists and how they can be studied to form a greater understanding of the past. As well as this, an obvious level of difficulty is that our understanding is based on the limited evidence base that's available. Even when there is a plentiful evidence base of archaeological finds, primary testimony and subsequent interpretations, there will be disagreement, conjecture and debate between groups who approach the past with fundamentally different perspectives on the world. In primary classrooms, sources of evidence are often broken into primary and secondary. Table 12.1 has a simple definition for each.

Table 12.1 Simple definitions that differentiate between the terminology. The sentences in bold are different phrases to describe source material that some schools use instead of 'primary' and 'secondary'

Term	An explanation
Primary source	A source with a direct connection to the specific history in question. This means that it is directly linked to what the children are studying. It could also be called a **historical source**
Secondary source	A subsequent interpretation of the history in question. This source is not directly linked to the original history and can use a range of primary and other secondary sources within it. It could also be called an **interpretation**
Sources and evidence	Sources are what remains from the past. They provide the historian with information to be examined and interrogated Evidence is gained as a result of interrogating the sources presented in the source material. The evidence is what informs the interpretation of the past and answer to the enquiry question

Table 12.2 expands on this by identifying examples of what could fit within each of the categories. As with anything history related, the nuance is key; it is very easy to tie yourself in knots over a specific example. Beyond this, it's important to remember that different types of source material are not directly comparable because they represent or record different things (this is explored later in the chapter).

Table 12.2 Examples of source material which could be classified as primary or secondary. Be aware that these examples are not an exhaustive list but rather a sample of what may be available

Primary/ a direct connection to the period	Secondary/ a subsequent interpretation
Artefacts	A historian's interpretation
A diary such as Pepys or the Wright brothers	A history textbook
A contemporary account	A biography
Photographs or film	A video documentary
Census returns or other data	An interactive classroom resource

THE ROLE OF SOURCES AND EVIDENCE

The acquisition of historical knowledge is achieved by studying a range of sources of evidence. Historian E.H. Carr wrote:

> As any working historian knows, if he stops to reflect what he is doing as he thinks and writes, the historian is engaged on a continuous process of moulding his facts to his interpretation and his interpretation to his facts. It is impossible to *assign* primacy to one over the other.

> (1961, p. 29, emphasis in original)

In the primary classroom, it's key to introduce children to sources and the concept of evidence at an early stage of their history education. This can be done by thinking in terms of what it is, the role it plays in developing and explaining our understanding and how collation is important. When appropriate, share the limitations of the evidence and that we do not have a complete evidence base, which means historians suggest and support instead of categorically proving something. Once introduced, I would always advocate for a scaffolded and instruction-led approach to enable them to achieve a higher level of success.

Once the children have been introduced to the concept, teachers can continue to develop their understanding of the concept and then how they can extract and interrogate information in order for it to become evidence. As they become more fluent, the scaffolds can be amended and withdrawn. Be wary not to do this too soon though given that the complexity of source material is hugely varied. Discovery learning can have a role once children have a secure understanding from which to delve further and deeper.

Instead of seeing this as an activity to complete and tick off on the spreadsheet, think of sources and evidence as critical features of the process of historical enquiry. A common misconception is that there is a single way in which to interact with sources. This isn't true and is the origin of my key mistakes when teaching in the past. Sources of evidence provide a snapshot of the past and must be contextualised within the sense of time, place, period and the overall enquiry question children are working towards answering. The children have had some introduction to the abstract historical world through world-building and historical fiction but, upon occasion, they need to be given specific context related to a historical source they are about to encounter. In the example lesson, Tacitus' account of Boudicca's speech before the battle of Watling Street, think about the difficulties children would have if they didn't understand the perspective from which it was written ...

'Bias' and 'reliability' are terms many teachers include within their history lessons. To begin with, it's important to identify the differences between types of historical source as bias is a consideration for some and less so for others. Think about the ruins at Lindisfarne and the Anglo-Saxon chronicle which contains an extract referring to Lindisfarne. They are fundamentally different in terms of what they contain and how they can support a particular enquiry question. In a 2020 video titled *What's the Wisdom On ... Evidence and Sources*, Christine Counsell explained the difference between relics of the past, which have no conscious commentary, and records, which do seem to have a conscious commentary (Burn et al., 2020). Bias is a feature of source material which is commenting on that period. A common misconception is that a biased source is unhelpful. This is an oversimplification of the truth for two important reasons: first, any conscious commentary will contain bias either explicitly or implicitly; second, the usefulness of a source is determined by the questions being asked of it. It is another reason why contextualising source material as part of the wider narrative is key.

HOW MANY LESSONS?

Here, there is no actual answer. The core considerations are how many lessons are available for the unit as a whole and the extent to which the sources offer knowledge that has been defined as core to the understanding. The use of a source may take longer than a singular hour lesson. This is fine when it adds value to the wider enquiry focus. Within the two worked examples, there are phases of the enquiry which provide room for manoeuvre. As Mary Myatt wrote in her 2020 blog, there is huge merit on doing fewer things in greater depth. What matters more than arbitrarily defining how many lessons to spend is enabling children to develop sufficient understanding. This can vary from year to year and cohort to cohort so professional judgement is key.

COLLATING AND TRIANGULATING SOURCES OF EVIDENCE

An important feature of studying history is collating varied source material in order to form a greater depth of understanding. As evidence is generated from sources, it should be collated and developing conclusions triangulated. This is where the teacher guides the pupils in making connections between the sources in terms of evidence found across them, contradictions between them and evidence that is only found in one or some. The evidence which is found commonly across the sources is what we can be more certain of. Teaching the children to collate evidence and triangulate findings using modal verbs to express the level of certainty is an effective way to support them in both understanding and expressing the fact we are rarely certain.

By doing this, children are repeatedly exposed to evidence across a number of lessons giving them the chance to get used to what they have learned, debate and discuss its content. This would make it more likely to be remembered. They are also being supported to think beyond isolated lessons and both use and apply knowledge. Every source is interrogated in relation to specific questions before the knowledge is committed as important towards answering the enquiry question. If this process doesn't take place, misconceptions over meaning may arise and go unchecked.

Example 1 – The extract in no context.

What does this source tell us about the raid on Lindisfarne?

Year 793.
Here were dreadful forewarnings come over the land of Northumbria, and woefully terrified the people: these were amazing sheets of lightning and whirlwinds, and fiery dragons were seen flying in the sky. A great famine soon followed these signs, and shortly after in the same year, on the sixth day before the ides of January, the woeful inroads of heathen men destroyed god's church in Lindisfarne island by fierce robbery and slaughter. And Sicga died on the eighth day before the calends of March.

The layers of understanding are easily missed if this approach is taken. What could be read as figurative may be taken as literal if appropriate direction and support is not provided.

Figure 12.1

SUMMARY

Think about your next unit of history and what you currently have planned:

- Is it clear what you want them to learn, as in know, or are you emphasising what they will do, as in tasks to complete?
- If you aren't clear about what they will learn, how do you know they have understood it and the lessons have been successful?

Creative and imaginative lessons are great but their value is hugely diminished if the children haven't learned something and been able to draw out the evidence from it. Some of the examples described at the start of this chapter would be great fun but would not inherently be a history lesson without a lot of adaptations. Instead, focus on how the wider curriculum (core and foundation) can supplement the core understanding from lessons deemed primarily as 'history'.

Remember, substantive and disciplinary knowledge play a key role in developing children's understanding of any subject so need to be careful considerations.

13

CONNECTING LESSONS TO FORM A NARRATIVE

BEFORE WE START ...

Think about your favourite unit of history:

- How did you think about sequencing the lessons?
- In what way did you establish and reinforce links across lessons even when the content changes?

WHERE I WENT WRONG IN THE PAST

The progression model has changed as was mentioned earlier in this book therefore I won't be denigrating my own practice too heavily in this section because what I refer to came from a previous time (little chronology pun for you there).

When I started teaching, the emphasis was not based around children knowing more and remembering more for foundation subjects. This was a considerable shift in emphasis from the updated *Education Inspection Framework* from Ofsted (2019). We were trained to ensure children had a growing skillset, with less emphasis on what knowledge was gained. While planning with the other teachers in the phase, we agreed which lessons each of us would prepare based around ideas such as daily life, military etc. Underlying narratives that would convey the coherence to children were not high on the agenda.

WHAT DO I MEAN BY FORMING NARRATIVES?

Your mind may first think about a story-based curriculum using fictional texts at its heart. To an extent, this is a useful place in which to start. Willingham's identification of stories as being psychologically privileged is something we can use to our advantage (2009). As you may remember from Chapter 8 on World-building, it is important to develop a sense of period so that the children can place specific lessons into the wider narrative arc. Ofsted's subject report, *History for All* (2011), refers to:

> an absence of coherence in planning the curriculum and insufficient links made between different periods so that pupils had little idea of a developing historical narrative; they found it difficult to build up a chronological overview and experienced history simply as a series of episodes.

This means that teachers should place the specific lessons within the wider overview. It is also a specified feature of the Key Stage 2 subject content. Beyond that, think about if the lesson sequence itself offers this sense of journey across the period and, if not, can this be mitigated at the start of lessons to fill in some important gaps. Within the two worked examples, the lesson sequences are designed to flow in two ways.

1. The enquiry questions are taught in a chronological sequence to support children to see how one flows into the next.
2. The lessons which make up each enquiry are designed to build on previous lessons where appropriate or work independently in order to not negatively impact the other lessons.

In the case of planning units of history, the narrative sets out which aspects of the periods are going to be studied in core knowledge. Beyond that it can be used to activate prior knowledge and help children to accomplish the curriculum objective for Key Stage 2 of 'establishing clear narratives within and across the periods they study'. A favourite quote of mine to consider alongside this is often attributed to Mark Twain: 'History doesn't repeat itself, but it often rhymes.' These rhymes are what we can exploit to enable children to identify the trends and contrasts over time.

A common phrase teachers hear now is that the curriculum is the 'progression model'. In 2020, Michael Fordham, one of the originators of this concept, defined it as follows:

> a curriculum sets out the journey that someone needs to go on to get better at the subject. In short, it *models* the progress that we would hope (although cannot guarantee) that someone will make. The curriculum *is* the progression model.
>
> (Emphasis in original)

This is a key consideration for thinking about the narratives the curriculum tells. If we do not actively consider and plan for the wider narrative arcs that run within and across the curriculum, the progression model can so easily lack coherence or, at worst, not accomplish what Fordham suggests it should. These may have been encountered as golden, knowledge or curriculum threads and aim 6 of the NC provides a starting point from which teachers can develop this coherence.

Once these broad-brush strokes have been established, they can be further sub-divided into small substantive concepts which are illustrated in the worked examples.

DIRECT INSTRUCTION

In Chapter 6, I made reference to Rosenshine's Principles of Instruction (2012). This is important when we think about teaching a series of lessons and not a series of lessons in isolation – specifically, principles 1 and 5 which are elaborated below.

BEGIN A LESSON WITH A SHORT REVIEW OF PREVIOUS LEARNING

This takes the form of retrieval practice which is explored below. In addition to activating prior knowledge, it's important to establish connections where they exist so as not to present children with a false narrative. For instance, if my lesson sequence studies the Roman invasion by Julius Caesar in 55BC and 54BC, I need to ensure the children know that the first was unsuccessful and the subsequent attempt was influenced by the failure of the first. However, if we approach the invasion by Julius Caesar in the same way as that by Claudius in 43AD we would fail to take into account that there is almost a century between them. Caesar had been murdered before Claudius was born.

Therefore, begin with a review of previous related learning and be explicit about whether the learning is directly linked in a causal manner, like the first example, or under the same substantive concept of an invasion. The role of chronology and timelines was explored in Chapter 10; using them as a graphic organiser, as Phillips (2008) suggested, supports the children in forming the narrative. Combining them with instruction-led teaching ensures the children are guided to make connections where they exist as linked events across the narrative or a broader substantive concept.

In the two worked examples, the review of knowledge is used to collate, compare and link information together to inform a more coherent understanding of the period or event in question. This is also an opportune moment to address misconceptions that may have arisen.

GUIDE STUDENT PRACTICE

The etymology of history includes the concept of being 'learned' and finding out/narratives. It is always important for teachers to remember that children are encountering a totally different world featuring completely different ways of life – as they may in fictional texts. The teacher is the narrator of the stories that the children are studying in history. We take them into the unknown and it is key that we guide the students towards a deeper understanding by being explicit about what information is core in individual lessons and then promoting the important role of connecting their prior learning and sometimes foreshadowing what is to come.

RETRIEVAL PRACTICE

Retrieval practice is an important facet of the children knowing more and remembering more, which is the current definition of progress in English education. Retrieval practice is an important factor in this because it is a way in which teachers can promote the importance of remembering what has been taught. Ebbinghaus' forgetting curve (1885) is a useful model to consider because it shows how learning information is forgotten unless we do something to keep it within our memory. By using low-stakes quizzes and other approaches, we can support the ability to both remember what has been learned and to draw upon it appropriately from the long-term memory.

Chapter 4 of Jones' 2022 book *Retrieval Practice: Primary: A Guide for Primary Teachers and Leaders* explores and explains the role of quizzes and the different types of question that they may include. When creating quizzes, I tend to balance the use of multiple-choice questions, including a correct answer and several distractors which are plausible, alongside short-answer questions which require a single word or phrase to be included. The nature of the questions is two-fold.

1. They ensure children have remembered information from previous lessons correctly. This can include challenging misconceptions from the lesson discussions or evident in books after initial feedback was given.
2. They make links to prior learning that will be relevant within the current phase of the enquiry or individual lesson. Enser (2020) wrote about a year-long project at his school: 'While the history questions were more likely to ask for the recall of dates or people's names, in geography, we would ask why or how something happened. This involves greater thought and, to use Fiorella and Mayer's term, it *generates learning*. Students were having to select information from their memories but also organise it to apply it to a new situation. They were, in effect, having to think harder' (emphasis in original).

As Jones (2022) writes, there are potential pitfalls of different types of questions and quizzes but promoting the importance of remembering is a useful endeavour. If the children have a knowledge organiser, these are also a useful tool for children to use to self-quiz. An important note to remember: low-stakes quizzes are *one* of many approaches to retrieval.

RELEVANCE TO PREVIOUS CHAPTERS

This can be built in to the sequence this book advocates for. The examples below offer ways in which narratives can be discussed, debated, embedded or extended, as described in previous chapters. There are multiple ways in which the teacher can support children to accomplish this so the suggestions are given as options. This chapter makes use of the long-term plan laid out in Chapter 7.

When introducing the enquiry question(s) for the unit of work, the children will have their attention drawn towards certain words and phrases which are key. The children will encounter these terms more than once through the curriculum. This is especially true of disciplinary concepts such as cause, change and evidence. In other instances, a substantive concept may appear repeatedly such as empire or others suggested in aim 3 of the NC. Think carefully about the number of times in which the children have encountered this and the nature of their prior exposures. If they have encountered the concept once, it may be worth explicitly stating they have seen it before and can use it to provide a clearer cue from which to draw in this instance. However, if they are more fluent, a more open-ended question could be posed such as: where have you used this concept before?

World-building is a useful vehicle through which to consider the nature of societies, cultures and more. When identifying the characteristic features of the period to be taught, introductory comparisons can be useful to draw out key trends such as polytheistic religions in the ancient world or the trade networks which were more expansive than children may presume. It's important to consider when is most pertinent to introduce these comparisons though. Too much, too soon is likely going to lead to confusion. A personal approach is to provide an introductory snippet or 'the gist'. This can be expanded upon and studied in more depth later in the unit.

The interactions between the development of humanity and physical geography were mentioned previously but core trends will be relevant. Think about the nature of settlements the children will encounter: which core geographical features are they located near to ... a river, the coast etc.? This is a common trend among settlements that flourish.

Chronology is an organisational tool to lay the taught curriculum together. The overall narrative timeline which depicts world history is designed to establish the wider narrative arc and therefore is a natural tool to build a coherent sense of time. This is also why I encourage teachers to look beyond the concept of concurrence and consider interaction as well. Not just the fact they met but when, where and how did they meet? How did those interactions proceed after first contact? Don't forget to support this with an appropriate map to add that all-important interdisciplinary understanding.

When identifying the types of source material the children encounter, a simple prompt can be included to identify the fact that the children have studied a comparable source before. Once again, this is simply adding in a cue to begin the process of activating prior knowledge in a disciplinary or substantive sense.

SUMMARY

To me, the key is not to think of the unit of history as a list of lessons but rather chapters in a story where settings and character arcs form the backbone of children's developing understanding. Call-backs and foreshadowing keep the learner thinking about the world beyond the individual unit in question.

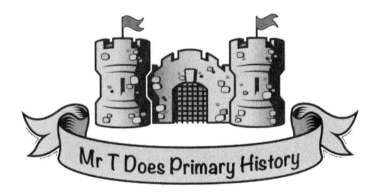

14

ANSWERING THE ENQUIRY QUESTION

BEFORE WE START ...

Please make sure that you have read Chapter 11 on enquiry questions and history lessons. This directly relates to that content. To put it simply, it's a lot harder to understand answering enquiry questions if you don't have an understanding of the nature of the questions themselves.

It is also important to consider the requirement of your school's pedagogical approach to teaching the foundation curriculum. The final product approach is common but the nature of the outcome can vary hugely.

WHERE I WENT WRONG

This is not just where I went wrong but, in the article from Ofsted titled *History in Outstanding Primary Schools* (2021a), it is noted as a common issue among a number of primary schools inspected.

> Inspectors saw some lesson activities that were not well-designed to secure pupils' knowledge. These included anachronistic writing tasks, such as writing a newspaper report on the Viking invasions of England, and activities that distracted from the history content pupils needed to learn.

There is nothing wrong with embedding historical knowledge in English lessons. It allows the children to access what they have learned and utilise it in different ways.

However, a history lesson should retain the sense of subject discipline where children combine the substantive knowledge with the disciplinary. At the end of each unit of work, as Riley suggested (2000), the question needs to be genuinely answered. If this doesn't happen, a core element of the enquiry question is missing. As a result, think carefully about what shines at the end of the unit of history. Is it the history, the English writing or the visual aesthetic?

WHAT THE CHILDREN SHOULD KNOW

The teacher should know the core knowledge base to be taught before the sequence begins. Therefore, the vast majority will be emphasised and embedded throughout the narrative sequence. If this isn't the case, the relationship between enquiry question, teaching sequence and outcome answer is weakened. A minimum expected knowledge base provides not only a useful reference point for teachers when planning and the basis for a knowledge organiser if one is to be used; it can also be a mode by which a summative assessment can be made. After all, progress is currently defined as knowing more and remembering more. How do we ensure they class has 'got it' if we didn't know what it was in advance?

As ever, a caveat is needed. Do leave room for manoeuvre as children being excited about the learning and bringing in outside knowledge is brilliant. The Ofsted research review stated:

> Knowledge is generative: it enables further learning. Pupils use their knowledge in directly discernible ways when they produce an outcome task such as an essay. However, pupils also draw on this prior knowledge much more often, and less visibly, when they make sense of new material. As they know more, they are able to learn even more, and more complex ideas, about the past. Therefore, this expanding knowledge is progress, but it is also a driver of further progress.
>
> (2021d)

From a seemingly simple primary input, children could start the journey to being a passionate future historian – Chapter 1 explained how it impacted me and look where we are now! Fiorella (in Enser and Enser, 2020, p. 7) wrote:

> Factual knowledge is important, of course, but we want more than that. We want students to *understand* what they've learned so they can apply their knowledge to new situations.
>
> (Emphasis in original)

Part of the role is to connect knowledge across units of work. This is not necessarily going to be evident in the final answer to the enquiry question but is a consideration throughout the teaching sequence. It is a reason why Chapters 9 and 13 contained careful consideration on connecting the history curriculum.

BUILDING UP THE KNOWLEDGE

Across the unit of history, it is important the children's knowledge base is ever increasing to form a richer and greater sense of period and in-depth understanding of said period. This is an important factor to consider when thinking about the final answer to an overall enquiry question.

At the end of each step of the enquiry (this could be a lesson or several with the same sub-question), ensure the children are clear about the knowledge which was core for that particular step. Personally, I ensure this is accomplished using a summary of learning. This can be produced in an age-appropriate way but it has the same question at its core:

What have we learned that *will* be useful when we come to our final answer?

The purpose here is two-fold:

1. to ensure the children know what the emphasis was in terms of substantive knowledge. This functions as a form of formative assessment
2. to provide a reference point for retrieval when the children come to think about what they should record in their final answer. It can be presented on a knowledge organiser or a focal part of the history display.

Table 14.1   How lesson summaries may look across school

KS1	LKS2	UKS2
A carefully structured conversation in two parts: 1) What have we learned today? 2) What is most important to remember for our enquiry question? The teacher writes key words and phrases that the children produce as a reference point This could then be turned into a sentence which can be scaffolded so they only need copy a single word or produce their own sentence The children are heavily supported on the difference between what they did and what they learned. The teacher may also turn ideas into the final sentence for them to read and rehearse chorally	Begin with the same process as KS1 because the content is vastly different This can be extended towards the children producing a linked series of sentences using a scaffold or an independent paragraph The difficulty here is that they shouldn't just recite what they have learned again but rather be supported in drawing out the key ideas. (They can absolutely use their books in the final answer as a reference point ... it isn't merely a test of memory)	At this stage, children will be well versed at producing paragraphs of varying purposes across subjects The emphasis here can shift from giving a minimum they must write to a maximum they are allowed to write. This prioritises summarising information and drawing out the key concepts It could be a small number of bullet points or a paragraph with a maximum permissible length

However it is presented, what matters is the important role of both reflecting on what the children have learned within that lesson and discussing the core role it plays in the overarching enquiry question. Table 14.1 shows an approach to how it can look in different phases across school. At its heart is this simple process: if the child cannot show this in English lessons, they are highly unlikely to manage it in the foundation subjects when they also have to focus on domain-specific thinking and communication.

WHAT THE ANSWER CONTAINS

Is a written outcome always necessary? No. History is often recorded in a written and oral medium. The curriculum outlines what children should be incorporating into their history work, some of which is relevant in the outcome answers shown in Table 14.2.

Table 14.2 National Curriculum content relevant to answers

Where it's found	What it says	Implication for teachers
Purpose of study	Teaching should equip pupils to ask perceptive questions, think critically, weigh evidence, sift arguments and develop perspective and judgement	A greater understanding of history is not simply recounting more facts. It involves consistent interrogation and correlation of source material Answers should include more than just a recount of everything the child learned
Aim 4	Use historical concepts ... to make connections, draw contrasts, analyse trends, frame historically valid questions and create their own structured accounts, including written narratives and analyses	In final answers, conclusions must be drawn using concepts to inform the nature of the conclusion. Written answers are an outcome and not the only outcome
Key Stage 1	They should use a wide vocabulary of everyday historical terms. They should ask and answer questions, choosing and using parts of stories and other sources to show that they know and understand key features of events	When answering the enquiry question the child must not only provide an answer but also what informed that answer
Key Stage 2	They should regularly address and sometimes devise historically valid questions about change, cause, similarity and difference, and significance. They should construct informed responses that involve thoughtful selection and organisation of relevant historical information	Building on KS1 answers, children must use evidence-led answers where their selections are carefully considered for maximum impact. Longer-form answers require deliberate consideration around what is included and how it is presented

The answer should involve the careful selection of substantive knowledge from what has been taught alongside the use of appropriate evidence, then drawing some form of conclusion using a disciplinary concept. It should not simply be a deluge of everything that child knows because not everything is intrinsically relevant to the enquiry question. Beyond that, curating knowledge and choosing the best possible examples promotes the importance of considering the relative strength of the account being constructed.

As the children's understanding develops, they can correlate and contrast the evidence to consider the relative 'certainty' of understanding. The evidence may suggest something but rarely will there be absolute 'proof'. This is a core part of the discipline of history to think about what has been learned but also the level of certainty around the interpretation.

SCAFFOLDS AND MODEL ANSWERS

Scaffolding writing is nothing new to children in the primary classroom. It is a feature of writing in English lessons and something that organises the children's knowledge to better equip them to produce an answer or end product. An important part of answering the enquiry question is the step that comes before … the plan of the answer. This is a chance to collate what has been learned, challenge remaining misconceptions and, importantly, organise the children's thinking. Caviglioli and Goodwin (2021, p. 28) wrote:

Without organisation, knowledge content is a mere list of discrete facts. But organising them through forging connections creates meaning.

Before writing the answer, a carefully organised plan using a pertinent graphic organiser helps with this process. Especially with younger children, this is most effective as a guided process as what they choose to remember as important is not always what we want it to be … Remember the school trip analogy.

Once the plan has been constructed, it can form the start of the assessment process. Consider the evidence children have chosen to utilise to support their thinking and the value it adds. This is a useful tool if the outcome is going to be oracy based (see below).

Popular scaffolds:

- structure strips used with a longer written answer to provide suggested content for each section
- the timeline is useful when the answer emphasises change over time because the answer, by its very nature, is underpinned by chronology
- Venn diagrams work effectively for a comparative answer to support children's ability to easily locate similarities.

THE VEHICLE BY WHICH THE ANSWER IS RECORDED

History is often communicated as both a written and oral medium. In primary schools, the need for evidence in books can mean the same medium is used across school. This may take the form of a formal essay, a double-page spread etc. being used across Key Stage 2 and in some cases introducing them lower. Turner (2022, p. 67) wrote: 'Achievement is the core purpose of our curriculum ...'; she goes on to list a range of outcomes across the curriculum that may not be found in workbooks or booklets and the potential disadvantages of only valuing what is written down. This is especially true when we account for younger children whose writing is so often at the earliest stages of development.

For written answers, consider what the children are fluent with during focused writing instruction lessons. If they are unable to write a sentence in an English lesson, having this expectation in the wider curriculum is unlikely to lead to consistent success. Consider the cognitive load to concentrate on the difficult challenges of the historical knowledge they need and want to share alongside knowing the importance of sentence or paragraph construction. Conversely, when a child is fluent with the English, the history task can embrace this skillset and it becomes a vehicle by which children can demonstrate their talents as a writer.

There are many examples of oracy-led outcomes that can be used effectively and are frequently shared on social media. Whatever the vehicle, the nature of the answer retains those core features described earlier in the chapter. Integrating technology such as green screens (easier to do than you may imagine) does not inherently improve the answer but rather provides a motivational factor for children. Table 14.3 gives several options I have utilised in the past, focusing on the knowledge it encouraged children to make use of.

Table 14.3 Possible outcome activities which embrace oracy and/or writing

Unit of work	Vehicle the EQ was answered using	Evidence used and interpreted
Ancient Egyptian achievements in Lower KS2	Green screen depicting the inside of a tomb from the Valley of the Kings	The Egyptian achievements related to burial and mummification Their culture linked to religion The role of scribes in this aspect of life Interpreting how different evidence can answer different questions
Anglo-Saxon and Viking conflict* in Upper KS2	A debate on the recorded perception of the Viking raid on Lindisfarne found in the Anglo-Saxon chronicle	The nature of who recorded the source material The limited nature of the evidence base Links to wider cultural beliefs and period of time
Various	Creating and curating a mini museum	Recounting the knowledge they gained through the unit of work Guiding the visitors towards what each display depicted including how that understanding was acquired and the extent to which this was a 'settled' opinion Additional writing task – creating plaques to explain each display

Note: * this particular example was part of the final answer and followed up with a more formal written piece for the UKS2 classes.

Before each of these events took place, the children worked to produce a plan of what was going to be said. This was where the teacher assessment took place because the plan revealed what the children had learned and deemed key to present. Children who struggled with English/writing were supported in various ways, depending on the logistics, but all the recorded ideas were theirs.

A word of warning though: just because the children had that information in their heads and understood it there and then it does not mean it has been embedded into the children's long-term memory. While the enquiry question answer serves as one form of snapshot assessment, it should be followed with further checks on whether the children have retained that information. Remember, progress is currently defined as the children knowing more and remembering more. Knowing it once is not the same as remembering it long term.

Mr T Does Primary History

15

MY INTENT WAS ...
NOW YOU CAN
IMPLEMENT ...

WHAT MY INTENTION WITH THE BOOK WAS

First and foremost, the intention of this book is to offer a possible approach to seeing primary history as more than an assortment of lessons about the past. The thought processes I have attempted to explain have evolved (and continue to do so) since the moment I undertook my first day of teacher training. They will continue to develop based on what I read, hear, see and encounter while talking to other incredibly skilful teachers and practitioners. The academic research, blogs and guides that I have cited are the ones that have impacted my thinking, teaching and pedagogical toolkit over time. They remain core considerations in the work I do.

Every time something new appears in the Twittersphere, History Association publications or as part of a CPD sessions I attend, the cogs start whirring in my head and the same questions come to the fore:

1. what about this is totally new to me?
2. what about this is going to change or tweak my classroom practice?
3. what about this ties into what I do already?
4. given this, where does my teaching go next?

None of this is ground-breaking. It's just what we teachers do. The best teachers I have ever met make the most of the new opportunities that arise. I didn't used to be one of them and, dare I say, had a somewhat fixed mindset. It didn't serve me well.

Where next for you is hopefully a question that's been at the forefront as you've read this book. If your 'to do' list exceeds five things, I'd reassess that list and reduce it down to the following steps. Why? In 2017, I was absolutely burned out. I had spent seven years trying to do everything. I was done with teaching and, to a large extent, it was my fault. It is so easy to think you are not doing the best for your school, class or self if things don't get done. Not only is it unrealistic but it is potentially damaging to your confidence, wellbeing or even health. Don't make the same mistake I did ... please!

Returning to the 'to do' list then ... Accept now, your to do list is too long, will not get done in full and revise down to what really matters from the book. Table 15.1 is how I attempt to structure my development targets now.

Table 15.1 Development targets

Something to implement immediately:	Something to implement ready for the start of next term:	Something to have implemented by the end of the year:

If everything goes swimmingly, you may have a fourth target titled in an ideal world, but think about how much else will arrive on your desk through the year. Simple, purposeful, embedded changes will have a lasting impact. A flash in the pan idea ... not so much. The plan for this book was to offer an approach to teaching primary history, which I hope you have enjoyed and taken lots from. Remember what I said right at the start, at the end of the 'About the book' section?

> Ultimately though, this book is designed to make teachers think. It's designed to make teachers think about what they teach, why they teach it and the value that knowing more and remembering more about the past brings to the students they teach.

HOW MY KNOWLEDGE AND UNDERSTANDING HAS SHIFTED OVER TIME

The 'Where I went wrong' sections have been cathartic to write. I've genuinely looked back and smiled, winced and giggled at what I used to consider made good history teaching. The reason they were included was not self-indulgence – otherwise I would have gone for me at my best in a 'just scored the winning try' pose. No, the purpose here was to highlight what we know deep down. Every single person in education makes mistakes at various points in their careers. Every single teacher has lessons where things just go wrong. In the same way that forgetting is an important part of remembering, mistakes are an important part of learning.

ENGAGING WITH THE HISTORY SUBJECT COMMUNITY

The history community are a wonderful and generous bunch. I've had the pleasure of meeting several of the people referenced in the book and their expertise has shaped the nature of teaching history for me. If you want to keep abreast of developments in classrooms and relevant research, Twitter is a great place to look, alongside membership of the Historical Association. I would absolutely recommend both in a heartbeat. While it can be a daunting prospect to join or engage on social media platforms, there are so many generous voices who are happy to help those that ask for it.

To get the most from the amazing history community, I have one simple approach that serves me well: never be closed off from the possibility that there is another way to do something and that it could be a great addition to your existing teacher's toolkit and knowledge base ... always be willing to have your mind changed. It sounds simple but it keeps your mind open, reflective and ready to try new things. Some will not go the way you want but others definitely will.

THE VALUE OF HISTORY IN THE 21ST CENTURY

The 2010s and 2020s have been a wild ride so far and that's an understatement of epic proportions. The news has been dominated by global conflict between East and West, a war of beliefs between contrasting ideological viewpoints, a pandemic causing misery and pain on so many levels and unpopular leaders in charge. Be honest, how many times throughout history could we say that had been the case?

History isn't just an arbitrary list of facts and nor should it ever be. Chapter 2, 'What is Primary History?', was the hardest to write because ... history means so much to so many. It is the all-encompassing narrative of literally everything that ever took place from humanity's earliest steps to now. History isn't going to be cancelled if we choose to teach new, varied and diverse stories.

Our understanding of the past is ever changing as is the lens through which we view it. The disciplinary aspect of history teaches children concepts and skills that are applicable in life. The importance of interrogating what you read, see and hear is key in a world where information is always available from dubious sources.

Last, but not least ... I adore history! I love encountering it. I love reading, watching, listening, smelling and just experiencing it in all its glory or, as Cromwell said, 'warts and all'. If we can help children to understand how the world of today developed over time, it sets them to understand how it exists today. No bad thing in my humble opinion.

16

THE FIRST FLIGHT: WORKED EXAMPLE

AN EVENT BEYOND LIVING MEMORY THAT IS SIGNIFICANT NATIONALLY OR GLOBALLY

KEY STAGE 1

When was the first flight and how do we know it happened?

How has flight changed since the Wright brothers' success?

ENQUIRY QUESTIONS

When was the first flight and *how do we know* it happened?

The role of **when** recaps the important role of chronology and how the new learning sits alongside what they have previously learned. *How do we know* is an introduction to evidence use. This is a foundational step on the discipline of history. Focusing on not just what happened but also how that knowledge has been acquired and the extent to which we are confident that this version of the narrative is as clear as possible.

How has flight *changed* since the Wright brothers' success?

The second enquiry builds upon the first by focusing in how the technology and role flight plays in everyday life has changed since the initial success. The emphasis is on how the children's understanding of flight came to be the norm – because it didn't used to be.

WORLD-BUILDING

Seeing an aeroplane in the sky or travelling on one is normal for so many children in the UK today. However, this is a recent change that they will not be aware of. It is out of their sphere of understanding. It is important to emphasise that the children will be learning about a world where aeroplanes did not exist and technology was very different (no mobile phones, no computers, no TV for most people etc.).

Geographically, the children should understand it happened in a different country to the UK and its position on a map. The physical geography of Kitty Hawk is important to understand why the Wright brothers chose it for their attempts. This would tie in with an understanding of: 'key physical features, including: beach, cliff, coast, forest, hill, mountain, sea, ocean, river, soil, valley, vegetation, season and weather'.

The second enquiry uses changes in technology to make links to the wider world including jet engines allowing holidays abroad for

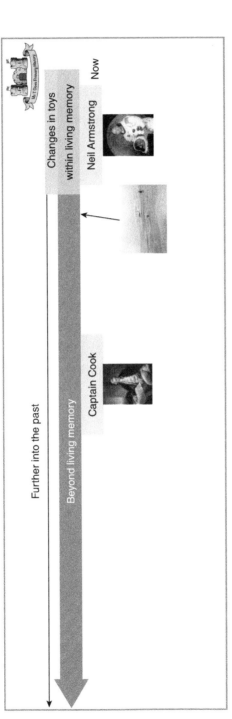

Figure 16.1 An overall narrative timeline which gives a chronological framework of a KS1 curriculum. The arrows represent a singular event and the bars a duration of time for a significant individual's life or changes within living memory

more and over longer travel distances. Radar and satellite navigation seen in cars started in aircraft and followed in spacecraft.

VOCABULARY

Chronological – before, after, then, next
  Source of evidence
  Continuity and change
  Aeroplane, glider, inventor, pilot, propellor, engine, rudder, jet, military, rocket

CHRONOLOGY

The event is beyond living memory and the children need to consider how this sits alongside the previous history units they have encountered. Use language to describe its position, such as before and after.

The internal narrative is important because the flight itself is on one day but the lead up to it is over a much longer duration of time. Once this date is secure, the children use that as a start point for enquiry two where the subsequent changes come after that. This can be done by sequencing the stages of development and counting on from one development to the next in months.

SEQUENCE OF LESSONS

Enquiry 1:

1. Introduce the children to the focus on flight and ask about their experience of it today. Explain they will be looking at the first time it happened.
2. Who the Wright brothers were and the development of their flier.
3. The day itself and how it was reported.

Enquiry 2:

1. Introduce the shift in emphasis and use the flier as a start point, focusing on how it was powered, what it was made of and the range.
2. Show a range of aircraft through time focusing on the same criteria to facilitate a clear emphasis on what changed, when it changed and how it changed flight.

Table 16.1

Substantive knowledge	Disciplinary knowledge
The first powered flight took place in Kitty Hawk, US, on 17 December, 1903. On that day, they made several successful attempts	Chronology – the event took place beyond living memory
The Montgolfier brothers had created a hot air balloon in 1783 but this had no engine	Evidence – in history, our understanding is made up by studying sources of evidence
The flier was designed by two brothers: Orville and Wilbur Wright. Their background was in other machines like bicycles and other motors	Sources of evidence – there is a range of sources that help inform our understanding (diary, photo, subsequent video, the flier itself). We use a range of sources to inform our understanding
Orville and Wilbur made notes which are still available for us to read	
They developed gliders first using ideas from other people. The development took many attempts across several years	
They made their own engine and propellors. It was important to keep the weight as low as possible	
It carried one person who laid down and steered it manually	
Five people witnessed the flight, including one person who took a photograph using Orville's camera	
Children will be familiar with the concept of flight from their own life experiences and what they have seen on TV or read about. The choice of explorer may have included someone like Neil Armstrong/Helen Sharman or Amelia Earhart/Amy Johnson who followed in more advanced flying machines.	

Table 16.2

Substantive knowledge	Disciplinary knowledge
Aircraft are now able to travel much further, carry more people and fulfil many roles for people (military, transport of goods, transport of people)	Change – change happens at different rates across a duration of time. Multiple changes can happen at once
Technology has changed to make them more aerodynamic; they have more powerful engines that use jets instead of propellers	Continuity – some aspects may stay very similar or the same over time while other aspects change
It is more common for people to have been on an aeroplane than in the past	
The concept of change over time was key when studying toys. The children will also be familiar with it from examples in EYFS and other subjects such as science and geography.	

ANSWERING THE ENQUIRY QUESTIONS

Enquiry 1: A sentence-level focusing on the fact we know the first flight happened because there are a number of sources of evidence including a diary, newspaper, photographs, the flier itself survives today and subsequent sources about it. The children should focus on what the evidence tells them and the fact there are multiple sources available. Enquiry 2: This could be an oracy-led task using motivational supports like a green screen.

An annotated version of the class timeline where the children can identify the changes that take place and how they changed flight. This could be at a word level or more developed sentence-level answers.

17

THE ROMAN EMPIRE
AND ITS IMPACT ON BRITAIN:
WORKED EXAMPLE

THE ROMAN EMPIRE AND ITS IMPACT ON BRITAIN

KEY STAGE 2

The Roman Empire and its impact on Britain

What was the Roman Empire and *how* did it become so powerful?

How did the Britons *react* to the invasion?

How was Britain **impacted** by the Roman Empire?

ENQUIRY QUESTIONS

Autumn 1: circa three weeks

What was the Roman Empire and *how* did it become so powerful?

Disciplinary concept: *cause*, by studying how the extensive road network and professional army supported the expansion and success of the empire.

This is the first time children have encountered an empire as a concept in Key Stage 2, therefore begin by recapping on the fact Britain had an empire during the reign of Queen Victoria – then highlight this is a much older example. *How* tells the children we are not asking if it became powerful because that is implied. The emphasis is on the causes of that happening. Cause is the second-order concept that will lead to the final answer.

The purpose of introducing the empire before Roman Britain is to ensure the children have a clear understanding of core concepts such as empire and its expansion, the military power of the professional army and political systems that changed over time. This is taught alongside a short geography unit focusing on the geography of Europe, including physical features such as the alps. This enables children to equate the Roman expansion and achievements such as the road network to a clearer geographic model. Meaning is generated via teaching the benefits and advantages they brought. This enquiry finishes when the Roman legionaries set foot on the shores of Britain – a cliff-hanger!

Autumn 2: full half-term

How did the Britons **react** to the invasion?

Disciplinary concept: **consequence**, by studying the different reactions of Briton tribes who chose to become cooperative client kingdoms and those that eventually rebelled.

Although not explicitly required by the National Curriculum, the continuous narrative of British history taught across Key Stage 2 means including this interaction between the Roman invaders and Britons, highlighting that there is no singular narrative to be told. It also bridges across what they already know from enquiry 1.

How was Britain **impacted** by the Roman Empire?

Disciplinary concept: **change**, by studying what the Romans brought to Britain as they settled. This is compared briefly to what the children already know from previously studying prehistory.

'Impacted' can be interpreted in different ways. We could study it in terms of changes brought by the Romans. This would enable understanding of how Britain was shaped as part of the empire. Alternatively, this could be studied in terms of consequences and what the consequences of conquest were. This is a more extensive study with embedded local links where possible. It focuses on the Romanisation of Britain and what the Romans brought to Britain from across the empire. In addition, it continues to build on the range of voices the children encounter by using pertinent examples that tell the narratives from a range of perspectives. Children will encounter concepts such as the purpose of roads and the concept of government.

WORLD-BUILDING

Enquiry 1:

As part of the first half-term which studies Europe and the Roman Empire, the children will have encountered the following locational and physical features which play a role in the expansion of the empire:

- location of the world's countries, using maps to focus on Europe
- physical geography, including rivers, mountains, volcanoes and earthquakes
- human geography, including types of settlement and land use, economic activity and trade links, and the distribution of natural resources including energy, food, minerals and water.

These links add contextual value to the expansion of the empire because it supports children in understanding the scale of task in creating such a vast network of occupied lands separated by seas, mountains and rivers. The purpose here is to emphasise why the professional army and extensive road network-building programme was beneficial.

Enquiry 2:

The purpose here is slightly different to enquiry 1 in that the emphasis is on retrieving prior knowledge about the Iron Age and using that as a stimulus for the concept of an invasion. This is an immersive lesson where the teacher leads the children through a script of what they should remember while building a model settlement. See lesson 1 of enquiry 1.

Enquiry 3:

World-building here acts as a way to link together what was learned in the previous lessons in order for the children to understand that the process of Romanisation took time to spread across Britain and they never truly had absolute control.

VOCABULARY

Chronological – period of history, concurrent, narrative, meanwhile, duration, interval

Source of evidence – primary/historical source, secondary/interpretation (see Table 12.1), historian, testimony, archaeology

Cause, consequence

Settlement, kingdom, client kingdom, annexe, province, rival, empire, monarch, republic, emperor, governor, infrastructure, invasion, conquest, rebellion, withdrawal

CHRONOLOGY

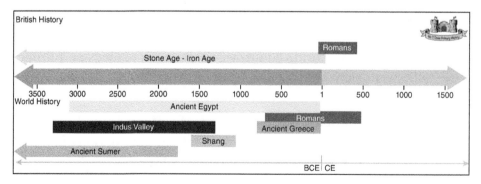

Figure 17.1 An overall narrative timeline for a taught lower KS2 curriculum. It gives a chronological narrative of British history so far and associated world history

Enquiry 1 – an overall narrative timeline to establish where the Roman Empire sits alongside the other periods that are relevant to the expansion. The children don't need to construct this but should spend more time discussing and studying it to establish links using the timeline and a world map. Specifically, the end of British prehistory, ancient Egypt and Greece end because they are conquered and become part of the Roman Empire.

Enquiry 2 and 3 – the same timeline is used because both enquiries are focused on Britain at different points across the period. The full timeline is constructed and interpreted at the start of the unit of work so the children can understand the rebellion they study is early in the period and before lots of Romanisation begins. The teacher can also draw their attention to later examples as the Britons rebelled on a number of occasions.

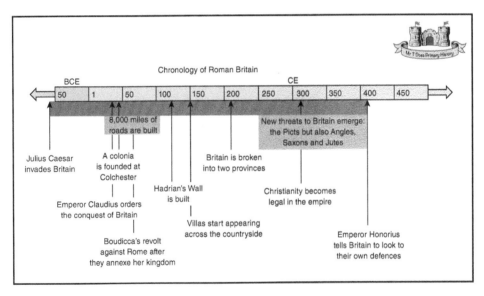

Figure 17.2 An internal narrative timeline of Roman Britain. The bars represent a duration of time and the arrows a singular event

SEQUENCE OF LESSON

Enquiry 1: The geography and history can be interwoven or geography then history can be studied in this particular example.

1. The founding of Rome myth and other possible options.
2. The expansion of the empire and the importance of infrastructure (roads, forts and settlements).
3. Benefits the expanding empire brought to Rome and its provinces.

Table 17.1

Substantive knowledge	Disciplinary knowledge
Rome was founded in 753BC There are a number of stories that explain the founding, including the myth of Romulus and Remus It took many centuries for the Romans to develop their empire The empire had territory across Europe, North Africa and the Middle east The Romans had a powerful army of professional soldiers. Their infantry was well equipped with a gladius, pilum, scutum, differing types of armour and helmets The soldiers built extensive road networks as their territory expanded The soldiers built many forts to defend from	Chronology – the Roman period covers both British and world history. It is concurrent with prehistory, ancient Egypt and Greece. They interacted with them too via trade and military conquest Cause – children understand that events in history have causes. They can be long or short term Evidence – we have access to written testimony from various sources and a range of archaeological sites and objects
Links to prior learning:	
Queen Victoria's role as the head of the British Empire.	
The concept of conflict and the role of the military via remembrance.	

Enquiry 2:

1. The various Roman invasions of Julius Caesar and then Claudius constructing the timeline.
2. The concept of consequence focusing on Boudicca and Cartimandua.

Enquiry 3:

1. Roman settlements in Britain at strategic points linked by roads.
2. Depth study – Roman York and what the archaeology has revealed about it. (York is a pertinent example, but use whatever is within your county if possible.)
3. Hadrian's wall and the varied people who lived there.
4. Legacy for Britain today.

Table 17.2

Substantive knowledge	Disciplinary knowledge
An invasion is where one group use an armed force to attack and take control of another	Chronology – internal narrative does not represent everything that happened. There are multiple stories occurring at once and we only study some of them
Britain was made of a number of tribes of varying size and power	
Some chose to cooperate and become client kingdoms (Iceni and Brigantes as a focus)	
Some chose to fight against the Roman invaders	
The Iceni initially cooperated with the Romans	
The king Prasutugus died and tried to leave half his kingdom to Rome and half to his daughters. Rome took over his kingdom.	Sources of evidence – Roman historians wrote about Boudicca's revolt and their accounts differ in some regards
Queen Boudicca rebelled and was initially successful. She razed several settlements including Londinium	
Cartimandua became a client queen	Consequence – the actions of people in the past had consequences for people in their kingdoms. Some were positive and others not
When the leader of the rebellion came to her for sanctuary, she handed him over to the Romans	
Her kingdom was attacked by other Britons and the Romans came to help her	
Eventually, she lost her kingdom to her ex-husband. Shortly after, it was conquered by Rome	
Over time England and Wales (modern names) were conquered but Scotland (modern name) was not	
The children have encountered the term 'monarch' when studying Queen Victoria and her role as a political and societal leader. This was also explored when thinking about opposition to a political leader during the short gunpowder plot unit.	

While not directly part of this enquiry, the children will also be taught that the empire came under attack from many sides and the legionaries eventually left Britain isolated and to look to its own defences.

Table 17.3

Substantive knowledge	Disciplinary knowledge
Some modern cities were key sites in Roman Britain. They were linked by the road network	Chronology – the conquest took many years to 'complete' and there were a number of rebellions against Rome
York was called Eboracum	
It was home to a legionary fortress which shows it was an important settlement	
The Roman Emperor, Septimus Serverus, ruled from York while campaigning in northern Britain. He was born in modern day Libya	Sources of evidence – testimony and archaeology exist from various sources across the period. We do not have a complete picture of this period
Many people lived in York, including the ivory bangle lady, whose remains were found there. She was African	

(Continued)

Table 17.3 (Continued)

In 122AD, Emperor Hadrian ordered a wall to be built to mark the northern border of the empire Many soldiers, including those from Africa, guarded the wall. The Aurellian Moors guarded one of the wall's forts near Carlisle Settlements such as York and Carlisle still stand in the same place today. London became the capital during this period and is the capital today (although it was not always the case). Some roads follow a similar path to that of the Romans' English features words which have Latin etymology Some of the Roman inventions are still useful today, such as concrete	Interpretations – focusing on how David Olusoga came to write about the varied people who lived and guarded Hadrian's wall
When studying the Roman Empire in EQ1, the children learned about the role of Roman roads and this continued in Britain. They also know the important role trade played.	

ANSWERING THE ENQUIRY QUESTION

Enquiry 1 – a short sentence-level answer which requires the children to answer the question with an explanation of what the empire was and reasons that enabled it to become powerful.

Enquiry 2 – a paragraph explaining what happened to one of the monarchs in question and the consequences of their choices.

Enquiry 3 – the most developed answer, which could take the form of a series of paragraphs, double-page spread etc. The focus is on the impact the Romans had on Britain, including both what the impact was and the evidence that informs that understanding from a range of sources.

REFERENCES

Adcock, S. (2021) 'Curriculum: The mirror and the window'. *Reflections on School, Teaching and Education*, 1 June. Available at: steveadcock81. wordpress.com/2021/06/01/curriculum-the-mirror-and-the-window/ (accessed 2 October 2022).

BBC (2016) *Slavery and the Cotton Mills*. 23 November. Available at: www.bbc.co.uk/programmes/p04hjyhj (accessed 14 September 2022).

Beck, I.L., McKeown, M.G. and Kucan, L. (2002) *Bringing Words to Life: Robust Vocabulary Instruction*. New York: Guilford Press.

Black, P. and Wiliam, D. (2005 [1998]) *Inside the Black Box: Raising Standards Through Classroom Assessment*. London: GL Assessment.

Burn, K., Counsell, C. and Snelson, H. (2020) *Film: What's the Wisdom On ... Evidence and Sources (Primary)*. Available at: www.history.org. uk/primary/categories/7/resource/9931/film-whats-the-wisdom-on-evidence-and-sources (accessed 15 October 2022).

Byrom, J. (2014) 'Progression in history under the 2014 National Curriculum: A guide for schools'. *Historical Association*, 29 September. Available at: www.exeter.ac.uk/media/universityofexeter/collegeofsocialsciencesandin-ternationalstudies/education/pgce/pre-coursedocuments/pre-coursed ocuments2021-22/Progression_in_History_under_the_2014_National_ Curriculum.pdf (accessed 15 October 2022).

Carr, H. and Lipscomb, S. (2021) *What Is History, Now?* London: W&N.

Caviglioli, O. and Goodwin, D. (2021) *Organising Ideas: Thinking by Hand, Extending the Mind*. Woodbridge: John Catt.

Counsell, C. (2018a) 'Senior Curriculum Leadership 1: The indirect manifestation of knowledge: (A) curriculum as narrative'. *The Dignity of the Thing*, 7 April. Available at: thedignityofthethingblog.wordpress. com/2018/04/07/senior-curriculum-leadership-1-the-indirect-manifes tation-of-knowledge-a-curriculum-as-narrative/ (accessed 14 September 2022).

Counsell, C. (2018b) 'Taking curriculum seriously'. *Chartered College of Teaching*. Available at: impact.chartered.college/wp-content/

uploads/2018/03/Christine-Counsell-article.pdf (accessed 17 October 2022).

Culpin, C. (2007) 'What kind of history should school history be?' *The Historian*, Autumn: 6–13. Historical Association.

Dawson, I. (2009) 'What time does the tune start?: From thinking about "sense of period" to modelling history at Key Stage 3'. *Teaching History*, *135*: 50–7. Available at: www.proquest.com/openview/f4b165e6b26feb9 7138f2b89facb2e49/1?pq-origsite=gscholar&cbl=48308 (accessed 4 October 2022).

Department for Education (DfE) (2013a) *History*. Available at: webarchive. nationalarchives.gov.uk/ukgwa/20140107091058/www.education.gov. uk/schools/teachingandlearning/curriculum/primary/b00199012/history (accessed 21 August 2022).

DfE (2013b) *History Programmes of Study: Key Stages 1 and 2*. Available at: assets.publishing.service.gov.uk/government/uploads/system/ uploads/attachment_data/file/239035/PRIMARY_national_curricu lum_-_History.pdf (accessed 1 August 2022).

DfE (2014) *National Curriculum: Alf Wilkinson on History*. 6 May. Available at: www.youtube.com/watch?v=SLhnL5Fc2wY (accessed 21 August 2022).

Dixon, L. and Hales, A. (2015) *What Makes Good Local History?* Available at: www.history.org.uk/publications/resource/8682/what-makes-good-local-history (accessed 12 August 2022).

Enser, M. (2020) 'Why some low-stakes quizzes work better than others', *tes*. Available at: www.tes.com/magazine/archive/why-some-low-stakes-quizzes-work-better-others#_=_ (accessed 24 October 2022).

Enser, Z. and Enser, M. (2020) *Fiorella and Mayer's Generative Learning in Action*. Woodbridge: John Catt.

Fidler, A. (2020) 'Embedding progress is historical vocabulary teaching'. *Primary History, 84*: 30–3. Available at: www.history.org.uk/publica-tions/resource/9753/embedding-progress-in-historical-vocabulary-teachi (accessed 24 October 2022).

Fordham, M. (2020) *What did I Mean by 'The Curriculum is the Progression Model'?* Available at: clioetcetera.com/2020/02/08/what-did-i-mean-by-the-curriculum-is-the-progression-model/ (accessed 14 September 2022).

Great Civilisations: The Vikings (2014) London: Ladybird.

Hales, A. (2018) 'The local in history: Personal and community history and its impact on identity'. *Education 3–13, 46* (6): 671–84. Abingdon: Taylor & Francis.

Hill, M. (2020) 'World Building: What can history teachers learn from imag-inary realms?' *in the olden days*, 28 April. Available at: intheoldendays.

home.blog/2020/04/28/world-building-what-can-history-teachers-learn-from-imaginary-realms/ (accessed 4 October 2022)

Hirsch, E.D. (1988) *Cultural Literacy: What Every American Needs to Know*. New York: Random House.

Historic England (no date) *Case Studies*. Available at: historicengland.org.uk/services-skills/education/case-studies/ (accessed 3 September 2022).

Historic England (no date) *Local Heritage Curriculum Planning*. Available at: historicengland.org.uk/services-skills/education/heritage-schools/local-heritage-curriculum-planning/ (accessed 3 September 2022).

Historical Association (2013) *The New History Curriculum 2013: Read It Here*. Available at: www.history.org.uk/ha-news/news/1715/the-new-history-curriculum-2013-read-it-here (accessed 3 September 2022).

Historical Association (2019) *Primary History Summer Resource 2019: Diversity*. Available at: www.history.org.uk/primary/resource/9647/primary-history-summer-resource-2019-diversity (accessed 3 September 2022).

Hodkinson, A. (2012) *How to Teach Chronology in KS1 and KS2*. Available at: www.teachprimary.com/learning_resources/view/how-to-teach-chronology-in-ks1-ks2 (accessed 24 October 2022).

Hutchinson, J. (no date) 'Knowledge organisers for primary: How to get the best out of them'. *teachwire*. Available at: www.teachwire.net/news/how-to-get-the-best-out-of-knowledge-organisers-in-your-classroom/ (accessed 23 October 2022).

Jenner, G. (2015) *What is History?* www.youtube.com/watch?v=dauxQKy IN4M (accessed 18 November 2022).

Jones, K. (2021) *Retrieval Practice: Resource Guide: Ideas and Activities for the Classroom*. Woodbridge: John Catt.

Jones, K. (2022) *Retrieval Practice: Primary: A Guide for Primary Teachers and Leaders*. Woodbridge: John Catt.

Le Domus Romane di Palazzo Valentini (2022) Available at: www.palazzovalentini.it/domus-romane/index-en.html#info (accessed 4 August 2022).

Lovell, O. (2020) *Sweller's Cognitive Load Theory in Action*. Woodbridge: John Catt.

Maddison, M. (2014) *The National Curriculum for History from September 2014: The View from Ofsted*. Available at: adamipsmith.files.wordpress.com/2014/04/maddison.pdf (accessed 14 September 2022).

Myatt, M. (2020) *Fewer Things in Greater Depth*. Available at: www.marymyatt.com/blog/fewer-things-in-greater-depth (accessed 14 January 2023).

National Trust (2020a) *Addressing Our Issues of Colonialism and Historic Slavery*. Available at: www.nationaltrust.org.uk/who-we-are/research/addressing-our-histories-of-colonialism-and-historic-slavery (accessed 30 December 2022).

National Trust (2020b) *We've Published Our Report into Colonialism and Historic Slavery*. Available at: www.nationaltrust.org.uk/news/weve-published-our-report-into-colonialism-and-historic-slavery (accessed 28 August 2022).

Ofsted (2011) *History for All*. Available at: assets.publishing.service.gov.uk/government/uploads/system/uploads/attachment_data/file/413714/History_for_all.pdf (accessed 27 October 2022).

Ofsted (2019) *Developing the Education Inspection Framework: How We Used Cognitive Load Theory*. Available at: educationinspection.blog.gov.uk/2019/02/13/developing-the-education-inspection-framework-how-we-used-cognitive-load-theory/ (accessed 15 October 2022).

Ofsted (2021a) *History in Outstanding Primary Schools*. Schools and Further Education and Skills (FES). Available at: educationinspection.blog.gov.uk/2021/04/27/history-in-outstanding-primary-schools/ (accessed 15 October 2022).

Ofsted (2021b) 'Chronological knowledge'. *Research Review Series: History*. Available at: www.gov.uk/government/publications/research-review-series-history/research-review-series-history#chronological-knowledge (accessed 22 October 2022).

Ofsted (2021c) *Geography in Outstanding Primary Schools*. Available at: educationinspection.blog.gov.uk/2021/05/11/geography-in-outstanding-primary-schools/ (accessed 21 November 2022).

Ofsted (2021d) *Research Review Series: History*. Available at: www.gov.uk/government/publications/research-review-series-history/research-review-series-history (accessed 23 August 2022).

Olusoga, D. (2021) *Black and British: An Illustrated History*. London: Macmillan Children's.

Oxford English Dictionary (OED) (1989) (2nd edn) *history, n.* Available at: www.oed.com/oed2/00106607;jsessionid=401719E958F8D9D0F0599 0F3A5FE8813#:~:text=A%20written%20narrative%20constitut-ing%20a,%2C%20people%2C%20individual%2C%20etc. (accessed 14 September 2022).

PDST (2016) *Graphic Organisers in Teaching and Learning*. Available from: pdst.ie/sites/default/files/Graphic%20Organiser.pdf (accessed 10 October 2022).

Phillips, I. (2008) *Teaching History: Developing as a Reflective Secondary Teacher*. London: Sage.

Quigley, A. (2018) *Closing the Vocabulary Gap*. London: Taylor & Francis.

Riley, M. (2000) 'Into the Key Stage 3 history garden: choosing and planting your enquiry questions'. *Teaching History*, 1 May: 8–13.

Rosenshine, B. (2012) 'Principles of instruction: Research-based strategies that all teachers should know'. *American Educator, 36* (1): 12–19, 39. Available at: www.teachertoolkit.co.uk/wp-content/uploads/2018/10/Principles-of-Insruction-Rosenshine.pdf (accessed 17 October 2022).

Severs, A. (2022) 'Including world etymology on knowledge organisers'. *Aidan Severs Consulting*, 22 August. Available at: www.aidansevers.com/post/including-word-etymology-on-knowledge-organisers?fbclid=IwAR1idqt6-_xH72NM5-ICHW6WlUSvBk-iXAaW32lTtPy0c4sFH_z4bzCoFq0 (accessed 29 September 2022).

Such, C. (2021) *The Art and Science of Teaching Primary Reading*. London: Sage.

Sullivan, R. (2018) *DfE Clarifies Reference to Enquiry-based Learning*. Available at: www.history.org.uk/ha-news/categories/455/news/3613/dfe-clarifies-reference-to-enquiry-based-learning (accessed 25 October 2022).

TeachMeet (2021) *TMHistoryIcons: Cogsci Special #TMHI*. Available at: www.youtube.com/watch?v=KEESb6xZ1tg (accessed 23 October 2022).

Turner, E. (2022) *Simplicitus: The Interconnected Primary Curriculum and Effective Subject Leadership*. Woodbridge: John Catt.

Wiliam, D. (2017) 'I've come to the conclusion Sweller's Cognitive Load Theory is the single most important thing for teachers to know' [Twitter]. Available at: twitter.com/dylanwiliam/status/824682504602943489?lang=en-GB (accessed 15 October 2022).

Willingham, D. (2017) 'On The definition of learning ...'. *Science and Education*, 26 June. Available at: http://www.danielwillingham.com/daniel-willingham-science-and-education-blog/on-the-definition-of-learning (accessed 2 August 2022).

Willingham, D. (2021) (2nd edn) *Why Don't Students Like School?: A Cognitive Scientist Answers Questions About How The Mind Works and What It Means For The Classroom*. New Jersey: Jossey Bass.

Wrenn, A. (2018) 'For whose God, King and country? Seeing the First World War through South Asian eyes'. *Primary History* (79). Historical Association. Available at: www.history.org.uk/publications/resource/9417/for-whose-god-king-and-country-seeing-the-first (accessed 16 November 2022).

INDEX